CONTEMPORARY'S

FOUNDATIONS
SOCIAL STUDIES

CONTEMPORARY'S

FOUNDATIONS
SOCIAL STUDIES

ELIZABETH ROMANEK

Project Editor
Cathy Niemet

CONTEMPORARY BOOKS

a division of NTC/CONTEMPORARY PUBLISHING GROUP
Lincolnwood, Illinois USA

Library of Congress Cataloging-in-Publication Data

Romanek, Elizabeth.
      Foundations. Social studies / Elizabeth Romanek.
            p.   cm.
      ISBN 0-8092-3831-4 (paper)
      1. Social sciences.   I. Title.
      H86.R66   1993
      300—dc20   92-36112
                                                              CIP

ISBN: 0-8092-3831-4

Published by Contemporary Books,
a division of NTC/Contemporary Publishing Group, Inc.,
4255 West Touhy Avenue,
Lincolnwood (Chicago), Illinois 60646-1975 U.S.A.

8 9 0 DBH 9 8 7 6

Editorial Director Caren Van Slyke	*Cover Design* Georgene Sainati
Assistant Editorial Director Mark Boone	*Illustrator* Cliff Hayes
Editorial Craig Bolt Lisa Dillman Eunice Hoshizaki	*Graphs* Creative Computing
	Art & Production Jan Geist Sue Springston
Editorial Assistant Maggie McCann	
	Typography Terrence Alan Stone
Editorial Production Manager Norma Fioretti	
	Cover photo © The Image Bank
Production Editor Thomas D. Scharf	Photo manipulation by Waselle Graphics

CONTENTS

ACKNOWLEDGMENTS

Photo on page 2 by John Fitzhugh/*Sun Herald*. Reprinted with permission of the Sun Herald–Golf Publishing Company.

Photo on page 4 reprinted with permission of UPI/Bettmann.

Passage on pages 4–5 adapted from *News for You*, December 12, 1990. Reprinted with permission of New Readers Press.

Photo on page 6 reprinted with permission of the Bettmann Archive.

Passage on page 6 adapted from *Aging*, by Alvin, Virginia, and Glenn Silverstein. Copyright © 1979 by Alvin, Virginia, and Glenn Silverstein. Published by Franklin Watts, Inc., New York.

Photo on page 8 reprinted with permission of The Image Bank, Chicago.

Passage on page 8 adapted from *Extremist Groups in America*, by Susan S. Lang. Copyright © 1990 by Susan S. Lang. Reprinted with permission of the publisher, Franklin Watts, Inc., New York.

Photo on page 10 by Kelly Carsten. Reprinted with permission of the artist.

Passage on pages 10–11 adapted from *Understanding Social Issues: Disabled People*, by Peter White. Copyright © 1988 by Aladdin Books, Ltd. Reprinted with permission of the publisher, Franklin Watts, Inc., New York.

Passage on page 12 adapted from *Southeast Asians*, by William McGuire. Copyright © 1991 by Franklin Watts, Inc. Reprinted with permission of the publisher, Franklin Watts, Inc., New York.

Photo on page 13 reprinted with permission of UPI/Bettmann.

Photo on page 18 by Lisa A. Dellert. Reprinted with permission of the artist.

Passage on page 18 adapted from *Lifestyles*, by Arthur S. Gregor. Copyright © 1978 Arthur S. Gregor. Reprinted with permission of Charles Scribner's Sons, an imprint of Macmillan Publishing Company.

Photo on page 20 reprinted with permission of The Image Bank, Chicago.

Excerpt on page 20 from *Remaking Motherhood*, by Anita Shreve. Copyright © 1987 by Anita Shreve. Reprinted with permission of Viking Penguin, a division of Penguin Books USA, Inc.

Photo on page 24, "The Emancipator," by Tom DeHaven. Reprinted with permission of the artist.

Photo on page 29 from the Bettmann Archive. Reprinted with permission of the *Akron Beacon Journal*.

Photo on page 30 reprinted with permission of UPI/Bettmann.

Song on page 32, "End of My Line." Words and new music adaptation by Woody Guthrie. Copyright © 1963 (renewed) Ludlow Music, Inc., New York. Reprinted with permission.

Photo on page 34 reprinted with permission of the Bettmann Archive.

Photo on page 36 reprinted with permission of The Image Bank, Chicago.

INTRODUCTION

Welcome to Contemporary's *Foundations: Social Studies*. With this book, you will build the reading and thinking skills you need to handle social studies material successfully.

This book is divided into five units:

▶ **Behavioral Sciences**, the study of what influences the way people think, feel, and act

▶ **U.S. History**, the study of past events in our country and how they are connected

▶ **Political Science**, the study of how governments work and the laws that guide them

▶ **Geography**, the study of places around the world

▶ **Economics**, the study of how people, businesses, and governments manage their money

The reading skills you'll be learning with this book include finding the main idea, identifying cause and effect, making inferences, detecting the problem and solution pattern, and predicting outcomes.

Foundations: Social Studies has special features that will help you build your reading, writing, and thinking skills. Keep your eye out for these:

Strategy boxes at the beginning of each chapter present a step-by-step guide for each new reading skill.

Pre-reading questions help you recall what you already know about a topic. They also pose some new questions to think about as you read a passage or look at an illustration.

A **Writing Workshop** at the end of each chapter gives you a chance to react to what you've read.

A **Post-Test** at the end of the book will help you see how well you've mastered the material in the book. The **Post-Test Answer Key** on page 154 will help you evaluate your answers. By filling out the **Post-Test Evaluation Chart** on page 155, you will see what skills you need to review.

We hope you enjoy the interesting topics in *Foundations: Social Studies*. We also invite you to explore the other books in Contemporary's *Foundations* series: *Reading, Science, Writing,* and *Mathematics.* We wish you the best of luck with your studies.

The Editors

UNIT 1
BEHAVIORAL SCIENCES

Behavioral science is the study of how human beings behave as individuals and within groups and cultures. What influences the way people think, feel, and act? What roles do people play when they are members of a group? Why do groups value certain ideas, customs, and traditions? These are some of the key questions that behavioral scientists ask.

The behavioral sciences cover a broad range of important issues facing you and other people in today's societies.

In this unit, you will study about people from various cultures and people of different ages and abilities. You will learn about prejudice and how it affects society. You will look closely at how families function and how work affects family life. You will also learn about one person's struggle to turn his life around from behind prison bars.

BEHAVIORAL SCIENCE
TOPICS

- Native-American Culture
- Achievements of Older Adults
- The Threat of Skinheads
- Aims of Disabled People
- Southeast Asian Celebrations
- What Is AIDS?
- Myths About Stepfamilies
- Baseball Players' Superstitions
- Working Mothers
- Reflections About Prison Life

AFTER READING THIS UNIT, YOU SHOULD BE ABLE TO
▶ FIND THE MAIN IDEA
▶ FIND DETAILS
▶ SUMMARIZE AND RESTATE INFORMATION

CHAPTER 1 | FINDING THE MAIN IDEA

News reporters write about people and events that will interest their readers. Reporters cover many topics in the behavioral sciences. For example, you probably have read news stories about social problems, human behavior, or a group's beliefs.

As you read a newspaper, the headlines grab your attention:

Mayor Launches Plan to Help Homeless

School Board Discusses AIDS Education

Clothes and Colors Identify Gangs

Study Shows Link Between TV and Violent Behavior

A **headline** is like a signal that announces the **main idea** of the news story. The main idea is a general statement that tells you the major point of a passage.

Based on the headline, you can predict what the news story is about. You expect the news story to give you more information about the headline.

Notice how the following news story explains the headline—the main idea—in more detail.

Powwows Keep Culture Alive

At hundreds of powwows each year, Native Americans come together to celebrate their culture. In the past, a powwow was mainly a religious event. The gathering was held when a tribe had a problem. Through prayers and dances, the tribe asked for help from the gods. Today, powwows are part religious ceremony, part dance festival, and part social event.

For Native Americans who have left reservations, powwows provide a link to old traditions. "When you move away to the city, you find out how important Indian identity is," said Phyllis Culbertson, a Native American.

Powwows are also a chance to link up with other Native Americans. Kay Culbertson, a Sioux, said, "To me, it's a time you see your friends and relatives from all over the country."

Native Americans see powwows as a way to share their culture with other people. "It's a good time to come together and educate the public," said Lance Richmond, a Mohawk.

Interest in powwows is growing. Tina Tromblee, a Cree, is happy to see this change. "When we were young, we were told to hide our Indian roots," she said. "Now, we are finding some pride in our culture and religion."

Many see powwows as key to their culture's future. "At one time we were forgotten people, but I think we're getting stronger," said Linda Yardley, a Pueblo. "From the powwow, we gain strength to go on into the twenty-first century."

From *News for You*, December 12, 1990

Let's look more closely at how the passage is organized. The news story contains six paragraphs. The sentence that states the main idea of a paragraph is called a **topic sentence**. The other sentences in a paragraph relate to the main idea. A topic sentence often begins a paragraph. However, sometimes the topic sentence appears in the middle or at the end of a paragraph.

▪ Can you find the main idea of the first paragraph in the news story? On the lines below, write the sentence that answers this question:
What is the major point about Native American powwows?

You were correct if you wrote the first sentence of the paragraph: **At hundreds of powwows each year, Native Americans come together to celebrate their culture.**

▪ Now go back and underline the topic sentences in the other paragraphs.
Did you underline the first sentence of each paragraph? If so, you found the correct topic sentences. All of the paragraphs explain the main idea— "Powwows Keep Culture Alive"—in more detail.

┌───┐

STRATEGY: HOW TO FIND THE MAIN IDEA

▸ Read the whole passage.
▸ Find the topic. *Whom* or *What* is the passage about?
▸ What is the main point that the author makes about the topic?
▸ Check to see that you have identified the correct main idea. Do the paragraphs of the passage explain the main idea in more detail?

└───┘

Exercise 1

Read the passage and complete the exercise that follows.

How do you feel about growing old? Do you think older people play an important role in society? Should people be forced to retire at a certain age?

A Lifetime of Achievement

Margaret Mead

People are not young and active at age 64 and then inactive a year later. In fact, studies have been done on many types of jobs. These studies have shown that older people are just as efficient as younger ones are. Sometimes, they are even more productive. And they are not likely to miss many days of work because of illness. Older people have a lifetime of experience to offer. What a waste it is when we do not use their talents!

Margaret Mead was a famous anthropologist. She studied the physical characteristics, the origins, the environment, and the culture of human beings. At 24, she made her first important study in New Guinea. In 1973, at 72, she returned to New Guinea to study the people again. Three years later, a TV crew filmed a typical week in her life. The crew followed her around during her busy work schedule. Soon they were exhausted from trying to keep up with her.

Pablo Picasso was a great artist. Working for 75 years, he continued to create masterpieces. He worked long hours that would be too much for most people years younger. He died at the age of 91. How much poorer the world would have been if Picasso had been forced to retire at 65!

Adapted from *Aging*, by Alvin, Virginia, and Glenn Silverstein

Circle the best answer for each question.

1. What is the topic of the whole passage?
   (1) wasted talent
   (2) older people's achievements
   (3) Margaret Mead
   (4) Pablo Picasso

2. Which sentence best explains the main idea of the passage?
   (1) Younger people are better workers than older people.
   (2) It is a waste not to use older people's talents.
   (3) A television crew made a film about Margaret Mead.
   (4) Pablo Picasso created many brilliant paintings.

3. According to the passage, what does *anthropologist* mean?
   (1) a person who studies the people of New Guinea
   (2) an older person who becomes famous
   (3) a person who has a busy work schedule
   (4) a person who studies people's cultures

4. According to the passage, why are older people considered valuable in many workplaces?
   (1) They work every day in spite of illness.
   (2) They have a lifetime of experience to offer.
   (3) They are willing to travel a lot.
   (4) They like to be kept busy.

5. Which fact is *not* given in the passage about Margaret Mead?
   (1) She studied the culture of New Guinea when she was 24.
   (2) When she was 75, she studied the people of New Guinea again.
   (3) A film crew followed Mead through one workday.
   (4) The crew became exhausted trying to keep up with her.

6. Which fact is *not* given in the passage about Pablo Picasso?
   (1) Pablo Picasso was considered a great artist.
   (2) He worked longer hours than many younger people.
   (3) He created masterpieces for 75 years.
   (4) He died at the age of 81.

Check your answers on page 156.

Exercise 2

Read the passage and complete the exercise that follows.

Do you know someone who has been the victim of discrimination? Why do some people form groups based on racial hatred, violence, and cruelty?

The Growing Threat of Skinheads

They shave their heads. They wear black leather jackets and combat boots with steel toes. Some tattoo their bodies with dragons, some with crosses, and some with symbols of the devil. They call themselves skinheads. They are gangs of teenagers scarring our society with racial violence and hate.

The skinheads' message is as hard-hitting as the baseball bats, pipes, and axes they use for weapons. They believe in white power. Racist rock songs, such as "Strong Free Nation" and "American Heritage," pound out their brand of patriotism, or so-called love for their country. A skinhead slogan says, "White revolution is the only solution!"

In the name of "white power" and love of country, some skinheads commit crimes against minorities. Their victims include African Americans, Jews, Hispanics, and Asian Americans. Their goal is to keep the white race "pure." Skinheads have beaten, stabbed, and murdered people. Their threat to our free society increases, and their numbers continue to grow.

Adapted from *Extremist Groups in America*, by Susan S. Lang

Circle the best answer for each question.

1. What is the passage about?
   - **(1)** minority groups
   - **(2)** skinheads
   - **(3)** gangs' fashions
   - **(4)** racist rock music

2. What is the main idea of the passage?

   (1) The clothes that skinheads wear show their cruelty.

   (2) Skinheads use baseball bats, pipes, and axes as weapons.

   (3) Members of minority groups are often victims of crimes.

   (4) Skinheads are teenage gangs who believe in "white power" and promote racial hatred.

3. What is the topic sentence of the last paragraph?

   (1) In the name of "white power" and love of country, some skinheads commit crimes against minorities.

   (2) The victims of skinheads include African Americans, Jews, Hispanics, and Asian Americans.

   (3) Their goal is to keep the white race "pure."

   (4) The threat of skinheads to our free society increases, and their numbers continue to grow.

Check your answers on page 156.

WRITING WORKSHOP

Brainstorm: Find a Topic

In this chapter, you read a news story about powwows in Native American culture. What religious or social events are an important part of your culture? What holidays do you celebrate with friends and relatives? On a separate sheet of paper, make a list of these special events or holidays. Review your list and choose a holiday or event to write about.

Focus: Write a Topic Sentence

What is the main point you want to make about the special event or holiday? Write a sentence stating the main idea. This is your topic sentence. Here are some examples of possible topic sentences:

▶ Thanksgiving dinner is an American tradition.

▶ Going to Mexican fiestas makes me proud of my heritage.

Expand: Write a Paragraph

Develop your topic sentence into a paragraph. Add sentences that explain the topic sentence in more detail. Remember, all of the sentences of your paragraph should relate to the main idea stated in your topic sentence.

CHAPTER 2 | **FINDING DETAILS**

When news reporters write a story, they ask questions that begin with these words: *Who? What? Where? When? Why?* and *How?* The answers to these questions are often the details of a news story. As you have learned, **details** tell you more about the headline—the main idea.

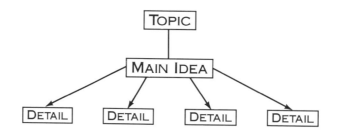

How can you use news reporters' questions to improve your reading skills in social studies? Look for the answers to the six questions as you read a passsage. This will help you find the facts and information related to the main idea.

Practice finding facts and information that answer the questions *Who? What? Where? When? Why?* and *How?*

■ As you read the following passage, try to **visualize**, or picture, the details the author uses to explain the chief goal of most disabled people.

Disabled People's Highest Aim

Most disabled people want to be treated the same way as everyone else in spite of their disabilities. They want to go where other people go. They want to use the same facilities that others use. In reality, most facilities have been designed for the average person. As a result, they are not available to those who have special needs.

Disabled people argue that things they want would suit almost everybody. They want wider doorways and less-heavy doors. This would be a great help to people in wheelchairs. But it would also be a help to parents pushing strollers or to people carrying heavy packages.

Handicapped people would also like buses and trains that are easier to board. This would make life easier for people with walking problems and for elderly people. People struggling with toddlers would also benefit. Spoken announcements in elevators and on public transportation would be good for blind people. It would also help the many people who have reading problems.

Adapted from *Disabled People*, by Peter White

....

■ Write the letter of the correct answer for each question.

_____ **1.** What do most disabled people want?

_____ **2.** Where do disabled people want to go?

_____ **3.** Why are most facilities not available to persons with special needs?

_____ **4.** How should buses and trains be designed?

_____ **5.** Who would benefit from spoken announcements on public transportation?

(a) because they have been designed for the average person

(b) so that they are easier to board

(c) to be treated the same way as everyone else

(d) blind people and people with reading problems

(e) the same places other people want to go

Here are the answers: **1. (c), 2. (e), 3. (a), 4. (b), 5. (d).**

Did you practice the skill of visualizing to help you picture the details in the passage? For example, were you able to "see" the images of people in wheelchairs and parents with strollers easily entering a wide doorway? The details paint a more complete picture of the main idea of the second paragraph: **The facilities that disabled people want would suit almost everybody.**

STRATEGY: HOW TO FIND DETAILS

▶ Ask the questions *Who? What? Where? When? Why?* and *How?*

▶ Visualize what the author explains in the passage.

▶ See how the facts and information give you a clearer picture of the main idea.

Exercise 1

Read the passage and complete the exercise that follows.

In what country did your ancestors live before they came to America? What special traditions, customs, and religious beliefs did they bring to this country?

Celebrating Tet—the New Year

In the countries of Southeast Asia, including Vietnam, the New Year is celebrated when the moon is full just before the spring planting. This is called the "lunar new year." It is a three-day festival that may fall in late January or February. The Vietnamese call it "Tet." It is a survival of old Chinese beliefs that probably **originated**[1] to ensure a good harvest.

All Vietnamese observe Tet, whether they are Buddhist, Catholic, or Confucian. A few days before the holiday, shops become crowded with people buying presents for their families and friends. The streets are ablaze with colorful lanterns and decorated booths.

On the eve of Tet, Buddhist families kneel before an altar. They pray for the spirits of their **ancestors**[2] and invite them to their holiday festivities. They also ask forgiveness for their mistakes.

---

[1]originated: began
[2]ancestor: one from whom an individual, group, or species is descended

Outside, fireworks are set off. In many homes, peach blossoms are cut and put in vases. There are decorations of gold and red paper everywhere. Children receive money in red envelopes. Special dishes are cooked and eaten. Tet is the most important holiday of the year. It is said that whatever happens on that day foretells what will happen in people's lives during the coming year.

Vietnamese Americans also celebrate Tet. In San Jose, California, for example, the entire Santa Clara County fairground is given over to the Tet festivities. People exchange gifts, visit with each other, and eat festive meals. American treats are sometimes added, and traditional sacred rites are often performed. For these new Americans, the Tet celebration is a link with life in the homeland.

Adapted from *Southeast Asians*, by Peter McGuire

Circle the best answer for each question.

1. When is the lunar new year?
   (1) when the moon is full just before spring planting
   (2) a few days before shops become crowded with people
   (3) the time for celebrating a good harvest
   (4) three days at the end of March

2. How do Buddhist families worship on the eve of Tet?
   (1) They hang decorations of gold and red paper everywhere and decorate the streets with colorful lanterns.
   (2) They give children money in red envelopes and serve special foods.
   (3) They buy presents for family and friends and serve special dishes.
   (4) They pray for the spirits of their ancestors and invite them to the holiday celebrations.

3. Why is celebrating Tet important to Vietnamese Americans?
   (1) It is a chance to meet in San Jose, California.
   (2) It helps them predict the future for the new year.
   (3) It is a link with life in the homeland.
   (4) It is a time for exchanging gifts.

Check your answers on page 156.

Exercise 2

Read the passage and complete the exercise that follows.

The enemies in the fight against AIDS are not the people who have the virus. The real enemy is the lack of awareness about the disease. What do you know about AIDS and the HIV virus?

What Is AIDS?

AIDS stands for Acquired **Immunodeficiency**[1] Syndrome. It's caused by a virus that destroys the body's immune system. As a result, the victim is left open to illnesses that a healthy person would be able to fight off. The virus that causes AIDS is called the Human Immunodeficiency Virus (HIV). If HIV enters the bloodstream, a person can eventually develop AIDS.

SOME FACTS ABOUT AIDS

- HIV is spread by the sharing of needles among drug addicts.
- HIV is also spread through sex with an infected partner.
- Infected pregnant women can pass HIV on to their unborn children.
- To avoid HIV infection through sex, don't have sex, or have sex with only one partner who isn't infected.
- Using condoms greatly reduces the chances of getting HIV.
- It is untrue that HIV is spread by mosquitoes.
- It is untrue that HIV is spread by hugs, handshakes, or kisses.
- Some people believe that a person donating blood can get HIV. That is not true as long as clean needles are used.
- A person infected with HIV may show no symptoms but can spread the disease.
- Once infected with HIV, a person is infected for life.
- To date, there is no cure or vaccine for HIV.

Answer the questions in the space provided.

1. Who can spread or get HIV?

_____

---

[1]immunodeficiency: not able to resist disease

2. How can an unborn child get HIV?

_____

3. In what four ways is HIV _not_ spread?

_____

4. What should you do to avoid HIV infection through sex?

_____

5. How can drug users spread HIV?

_____

Check your answers on page 156.

WRITING WORKSHOP

Brainstorm: Ask News Reporters' Questions

In this chapter, you read about Vietnamese Americans, a group of recent American immigrants. Gather facts and details about your own ancestors. Ask the kind of questions a news reporter would ask, beginning with _Who? What? Where? When? Why?_ and _How?_ Some examples are listed below.

▶ When did your ancestors arrive in the United States?

▶ Why did they want to come here?

▶ Where did they come from?

▶ What foods, customs, or celebrations remind you of your ancestors?

▶ How did they cope with being strangers in a new country?

Focus: Make a List of Facts

Write the answers to your questions. You might want to ask family members to help you. Then organize your answers into a list. Use the list of facts about AIDS on page 14 as a model. Think of a title to describe your list.

Expand: Write a Paragraph

Write a topic sentence to begin a paragraph about your ancestors. Then use your list of facts to write about the details.

CHAPTER 3 | RESTATING AND SUMMARIZING

How do you decide which TV show to watch? You probably look through the TV listings in the newspaper and read the summaries:

> **April James**—Guests discuss relationships between stepmothers and stepdaughters.
>
> **Saturday Morning News Special**—Anchorman Peter Kent explains prejudice to young viewers. He uses a skeleton to show that underneath the skin all humans are alike.
>
> **The American Experience**—Americans' love of baseball is examined. Fans explain why baseball players are heroes.

These descriptions summarize the TV shows in one or two sentences. They give you a general idea of what these programs are about.

A **summary** briefly tells you the most important ideas and details about a subject.

As you read the following passage, notice that the first paragraph summarizes "Cinderella," a well-known fairy tale.

Myths About Stepfamilies

After Cinderella's mother dies, her father remarries. Cinderella's new stepmother and two stepsisters treat her cruelly. Jealous of Cinderella's goodness and beauty, they make her suffer. They call her names and order her around. They force her to do impossible tasks. The stepmother forbids Cinderella to attend the king's ball. Her fairy godmother comes to her rescue. Cinderella goes to the party. There she meets a handsome prince. At the end of the story, Cinderella triumphs over her wicked stepfamily. She marries the prince, and they live happily ever after.

Some people have a negative view of stepfamilies, based on "Cinderella" and other fairy tales. However, do these stories paint a true picture? Are real-life stepparents wicked and mean? Are stepchildren rejected, alone, or mistreated? Are members in a stepfamily always jealous of one another?

Stepfamilies form because of remarriage after a divorce or the death of a parent. Grieving the loss of the first family and adjusting to the new one creates conflict and tension. A parent's remarriage is unsettling. Yet today's stepfamilies are not doomed to failure. Many children and adults are combining two families and making the effort succeed.

· ·

In the summary of "Cinderella," many of the details of the original story are not included. The author has selected only the most important ideas and details. She identifies the major characters, summarizes their actions, and explains the ending of the story. The author does not use the exact words from the fairy tale. Instead, she restates the main points in her own words. **Restating** means using different words to explain the same information in another way. Restating and summarizing information helps you better understand what you read.

■ Practice your skill at restating information. Reread the third paragraph of the passage about stepfamilies. Then answer this question in your own words.

Why do stepfamilies form?

_____

_____

You might have answered: **because one parent remarries after he or she gets a divorce or a husband or wife dies.** Your words may be different, but your answer should state the same information.

STRATEGY: HOW TO SUMMARIZE AND RESTATE INFORMATION

▶ Read the whole passage carefully.
▶ Find the topic, main points, and most important details. *Whom* or *What* is the passage about? What does the author tell you about the topic?
▶ Use your own words to explain the information.
▶ Check to see that you have summarized or restated the information accurately. Does your explanation of ideas and details match the information in the original passage?

Exercise 1

Read the passage and complete the exercise that follows.

Do you think Friday the 13th is an unlucky day? Since early times, people have believed that certain objects or actions bring good luck or bad luck. How do such beliefs affect human behavior?

Some Baseball Players' Superstitions

Superstitions are beliefs in the supernatural that not everyone shares. One person's superstitions are another person's nonsense.

In America, baseball players, racing car drivers, test pilots, sky divers, and lovers are said to be highly superstitious. In a baseball game, once the ball leaves the pitcher's hand, no one can predict the outcome. A pitcher may throw his best curveball and see it go sailing over the fence for a grand-slam home run. A pitcher may perform any number of superstitious acts. He might tug at his cap. He might smooth the dirt around the mound. Or he might touch the resin bag. These are ways that a pitcher seeks to control the uncertainty of the game.

Hitters also have superstitious practices. Hitting is often a matter of chance. Luck plays a part in whether the ball will plunk right into a waiting glove or fly down the baseline for a double. One former big-league player described how he hoped to keep a batting streak going. "I once ate fried chicken every day at 4 P.M., kept my eyes closed during the national anthem, and changed sweatshirts at the end of the fourth inning for seven consecutive nights—until the streak ended."

Adapted from *Lifestyles*, by Arthur S. Gregor

Circle the best answer for each question.

1. What is the topic of the entire passage?

    (1) pitching styles

    (2) winning streaks

    (3) superstitions of baseball players

    (4) lucky hitters

2. Which sentence most accurately restates the last sentence of the second paragraph?

    (1) Predicting the outcome of a baseball game helps pitchers throw better curveballs.

    (2) Performing certain actions helps pitchers feel more in control of what happens during a game.

    (3) Avoiding home runs helps pitchers conquer their fears of losing a game.

    (4) Being afraid of bad luck makes pitchers behave nervously.

3. Which sentence best summarizes the main point of the third paragraph?

    (1) One player ate fried chicken every day at 4 P.M. to bring luck.

    (2) Batters perform superstitious acts to improve their batting averages.

    (3) A baseball player hits a fly ball because he has bad luck.

    (4) Eating certain foods and changing clothes helps a batter hit more balls.

4. Which of the following actions that players do to bring luck are mentioned in the passage? **You may check (✓) more than one.**

    _____ **(1)** A player closes his eyes during the national anthem.

    _____ **(2)** A player wears his hat backwards.

    _____ **(3)** A player changes his sweatshirt at the end of the fourth inning for seven nights in a row.

    _____ **(4)** A player touches the resin bag.

    _____ **(5)** A player stamps his feet three times before he pitches the ball.

Check your answers on page 156.

Exercise 2

Read the passage and complete the exercise that follows.

How does working affect a woman's role as a wife and mother? What effects do working mothers have on family life? In the following passage, Pat, a thirty-one-year-old salesperson, discusses her feelings about working.

A Working Mother

I would like my daughter, who is four, to grow up very prepared and very directed. I think it's important that she sees me as a working woman and that she understands what I do. I take her to **accounts**[1] with me once a week. She has a comprehension of what it is that I do. I don't think she understands what her father does, however. He's in sales, too, but he doesn't feel comfortable taking her with him on calls. Somehow, in this culture, it's still more acceptable for the woman to bring her child along than it is for the man.

I think it's important, too, that she understands the economic reason why a mother works. I like her to know that both her father and I contribute to the **economic welfare**[2] of the family. She understands that my working brings in an income, and that's important for her to know. Hey, we need the money. That's a fact.

Her father and I share child-rearing and household tasks. Peter, for example, does all his own ironing each morning before work. She watches cartoons while I'm doing my exercises, and Peter's right there with her doing the ironing. She's going to grow up thinking that fathers do the ironing, I'm sure.

Excerpted from *Remaking Motherhood*, by Anita Shreve

[1]**accounts:** customers
[2]**economic welfare:** financial well-being

Answer the questions in the space provided.

1. In the second paragraph, Pat describes one of the reasons why a mother works. In your own words, summarize the reason.

_____

_____

2. The passage concludes with a scene from Pat's family life. In your own words, restate what each family member is doing.

_____

_____

3. Why does the mother bring her daughter to work with her once a week when she calls on her customers? **Circle the best answer.**

(1) so that her daughter will choose to be in sales when she grows up

(2) to show her daughter how to meet people

(3) so that her daughter understands what her mother does when she works

(4) to show her daughter that it is better to work than to stay at home

Check your answers on page 156.

WRITING WORKSHOP

Brainstorm: Make a List

You just read Pat's summary of her daily activities. What routine tasks do you perform at home or on your job each day? Make a list of all your tasks and responsibilities.

Focus: Select the Most Important Details

Review your list. Which tasks are most important? What are your major responsibilities? Underline your most important tasks and responsibilities.

Expand: Write a Summary

Write a paragraph summarizing your most important tasks and responsibilities.

UNIT 1
REVIEW

Read the passage and complete the exercise that follows.

What is your view of prison life? Do you think that criminals can change their behavior?

Etheridge Knight: Prison-Born Poet

In 1960, Etheridge Knight committed a robbery. Knight was a drug addict. He snatched a woman's purse to get money for his habit. Following his arrest, he was convicted. His sentence was ten to twenty-five years in Indiana State Prison.

Recalling that time, Knight said, "There had to be something better for me in life than a ten- to twenty-five-year sentence stretched endlessly before me." He found that the best escape from prison life was education. He spent his time studying books on a variety of subjects—art, science, and religion. Through reading, he gained a sense of self-worth—his value as a human being. Reading also gave Knight the tools he needed to become a writer.

Knight wrote about himself and prison life. He spoke out against social injustice to African Americans. Thus, he became a voice for African-American prisoners. Writing led Knight to the feelings he had hoped to find through drugs. Writing allowed him to communicate. It was a way to express himself without breaking the law. Knight's first book, *Poems from Prison*, was published in 1968. Gwendolyn Brooks, a famous African-American poet, wrote the introduction to this book. She said, "This poetry is a major announcement."

Knight once summed up his life. Part of it had been spent as an American soldier during the Korean War. He said, "I died in Korea from a **shrapnel**[1] wound, and narcotics **resurrected**[2] me. I died from a prison sentence, and poetry brought me back to life."

---

[1]shrapnel: metal pieces from an exploded bomb, shell, or mine
[2]resurrected: brought back to life

Circle the best answer for each question.

1. What is the main idea of the first paragraph?
   (1) Etheridge Knight committed a robbery and was sentenced to several years in jail.
   (2) Etheridge Knight was a drug addict.
   (3) Etheridge Knight snatched a woman's purse.
   (4) Etheridge Knight needed money for his drug habit.

2. Which definition best restates the meaning of *self-worth*?
   (1) the value of religion in a person's life
   (2) the recognition of one's importance as a person
   (3) the act of educating yourself
   (4) the knowledge gained by reading books on art

3. According to the third paragraph, Etheridge Knight did *not* write about
   (1) himself
   (2) prison life
   (3) social injustice
   (4) drug laws

4. According to Etheridge Knight's summary of his life (paragraph 4), what most influenced his life in a positive way?
   (1) the Korean War
   (2) his war injury
   (3) his drug addiction
   (4) his love of poetry

5. The title of the passage means that Knight
   (1) was born in prison, not in a hospital
   (2) found a new life as a writer while in prison
   (3) was destined as a child to go to prison
   (4) was a born-again Christian

Check your answers on page 156.

UNIT 2
U.S. HISTORY

What is history? History is a record of past events. Historians are people who study and explore the past. They examine the relationships between events. They look at the conditions, people, and ideas connected to events. Like sports announcers, historians see the action from a distance. Historians notice the important players who influence situations. The actions of both heroes and villains have shaped the course of history.

U.S. HISTORY

TOPICS

- Historic Moments on TV
- Pioneers of Flight
- The Montgomery Bus Boycott
- The Dust Bowl
- How Labor Unions Began
- Cowboys in the Wild West
- How the Car Changed America
- The Role of Civil Disobedience
- How Prohibition Failed
- The Trail of Tears
- President Roosevelt Tackles a Problem
- The Father's Changing Role
- Comparing Rosie the Riveter and June Cleaver
- Learning a Lesson from Lincoln
- Comparing Booker T. Washington and W. E. B. Du Bois
- The Power of Writing

AFTER READING THIS CHAPTER, YOU SHOULD BE ABLE TO UNDERSTAND

▶ SEQUENCE

▶ CAUSE AND EFFECT

▶ PROBLEM AND SOLUTION

▶ COMPARISON AND CONTRAST

CHAPTER 4 | SEQUENCE

Imagine hearing a sports announcer giving this play-by-play account during a baseball game:

> The pitcher leans forward and waits for the signal from the catcher. Here's the windup and the pitch. The batter swings and hits a high pop fly. The outfielder catches it easily. One out.

Sports announcers describe each action in **sequence**, or time order. They tell you what happened first, what happened next, and so on. As a result, you can easily follow the events of a game.

Knowing the order in which events occurred will also help you better understand history. Many historical accounts, like play-by-play accounts, report a related series of actions or events. History tells a story in which events are often linked together in a sequence.

■ Do you recall watching an event reported on TV that made history? Were you glued to your TV set as the story unfolded? As you read the following passage, underline the dates and word clues that signal time order.

Historic Moments on TV

TV has the power to bring history into your living room. You can witness the events as they happen. What are some historic moments that Americans have viewed on their TV sets?

In November 1963, President John F. Kennedy's murder shocked the country. Every TV station broadcast this national tragedy, beginning with the fateful shooting in Dallas and ending with the funeral. Millions of Americans watched and grieved.

From 1965 to 1973, the six o'clock news featured scenes from the Vietnam War. For the first time, TV audiences saw the reality of active combat. Each night, TV sets carried violent images of soldiers fighting in this long, unpopular war. Finally, on January 27, 1973, the United States and North Vietnam signed a cease-fire agreement.

In July 1969, Americans stared at their TV sets in amazement as astronauts Neil Armstrong and Buzz Aldrin walked on the moon and made history. Then TV viewers heard Neil Armstrong's famous statement: "That's one small step for a man, one giant leap for mankind."

In January 1991, people once again witnessed America's involvement in a war overseas. During the Persian Gulf War, TV screens showed missiles bursting in the air over Baghdad. Americans also listened to live interviews with soldiers, both men and women. Television makes history an immediate experience.

• •

Did you underline the date of each event? Other words that signaled time order are *first*, *beginning*, *ending*, and *then*. You can summarize the sequence of events in the passage by creating a **time line**. A time line is a line or bar labeled with dates and key events.

■ Fill in the missing information in the time line based on the passage.

1963	1969	1973	1991
President Kennedy murdered			

Compare your time line with the one below.

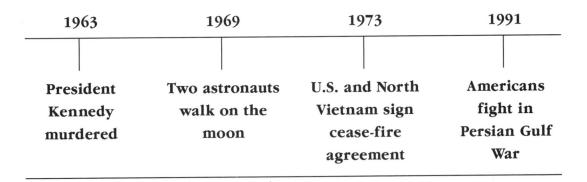

1963	1969	1973	1991
President Kennedy murdered	Two astronauts walk on the moon	U.S. and North Vietnam sign cease-fire agreement	Americans fight in Persian Gulf War

STRATEGY: HOW TO UNDERSTAND SEQUENCE

▶ Find the topic. What historical event or time period is described?
▶ Look for clue words that help you organize the sequence. Examples include dates and words such as *next*, *before*, *later*, *after*, and *finally*.
▶ If possible, create a time line to summarize the events.
▶ Check to see how the series of events is related.

Exercise 1

Read the passage and complete the exercise that follows.

Since ancient times, people have dreamed of flying. What famous Americans made this dream come true? Who are some heroes in the history of flight?

Pioneers of Flight

Each of these newspaper headlines hails a feat in the history of flight.

"Flying Machine Soars Three Miles in Teeth of High Wind"
"Millions Roar Welcome to Lindbergh"
"Amelia Earhart Flies Across Ocean"

On December 17, 1903, a crowd gathered on a windy beach near Kitty Hawk, North Carolina. Orville Wright watched as his brother, Wilbur, steered the flying machine they had both designed. Wilbur soared like a bird in the amazing invention. This first plane was powered by a gas engine. "It's a success!" Orville said after Wilbur flew the first mile. Then Wilbur glided in the air for two more miles before he finally landed the plane.

On May 20, 1927, Charles Lindbergh climbed into the cockpit of his plane. He had named it the *Spirit of St. Louis*. Taking off from New York, he arrived in Paris thirty-three and a half hours later. He was the first man to make a solo, nonstop flight across the Atlantic Ocean. One newspaper called this "the greatest feat of a **solitary**[1] man in the records of the human race." Fans flocked to parades. They welcomed home their new American hero—"Lucky Lindy."

Exactly five years later, another pilot made history. Her name was Amelia Earhart. On the night of May 20, 1932, she took off from Newfoundland in a red, single-engine plane. After a very dangerous flight, she landed in Ireland fifteen hours later. Earhart was the first woman to fly across the Atlantic Ocean alone. She said, "I hope that the flight meant something to women in **aviation**.[2] If it has, I shall feel it was **justified**."[3] She soon became known as "Lady Lindy, First Lady of the Air."

---

[1]**solitary:** alone
[2]**aviation:** the operation of aircraft
[3]**justified:** shown to be reasonable

Charles Lindbergh

Answer the questions in the space provided.

1. Fill in the events on the time line.

December 17, 1903	May 20, 1927	May 20, 1932

_____ _____ _____

_____ _____ _____

_____ _____ _____

_____

2. Why do you think Amelia Earhart was nicknamed ''Lady Lindy''?

_____

3. Why was the Wright Brothers' three-mile flight so important?

_____

Check your answers on page 157.

Exercise 2

Read the passage and complete the exercise that follows.

In the 1950s, Montgomery, Alabama's public bus system was racially segregated. Bus drivers could order African Americans to give up their seats to white people. Would you have given up your seat?

The Montgomery Bus Boycott

Rosa Parks

On Thursday, December 1, 1955, Rosa Parks boarded a bus in Montgomery, Alabama. She sat down in the first row of the middle section of seats. This area was open to blacks if all whites were seated. At the next stop, some whites got on. They filled all the "whites-only" seats. But one white man was left standing.

Then, the bus driver, James Blake, said, "Y'all better make it light on yourself and let me have those seats." Three black people rose, but Rosa Parks didn't budge.

"When he saw me still sitting," Parks recalled, "he asked if I was going to stand up, and I said, 'No, I'm not.' " Blake replied, "Well, if you don't stand up, I'm going to have to call the police and have you arrested." Parks said, "You may do that." Moments later, a police car took Parks to the county jail. She was charged with breaking the law.

News of her arrest spread quickly. E. D. Nixon, a former head of the **NAACP**,[1] called Reverend Ralph Abernathy on Friday morning, December 2. They arranged a meeting with other black ministers and leaders for Friday evening. At the meeting, most agreed to boycott, or not ride, the buses for one day.

On Monday morning, December 5, a torn piece of cardboard appeared at the main downtown bus stop. It said: "PEOPLE DON'T RIDE THE BUSES TODAY. DON'T RIDE FOR FREEDOM." The one-day boycott was a success.

---

¹NAACP: National Association for the Advancement of Colored People

Ministers and community leaders met again that afternoon and chose a new leader—Dr. Martin Luther King, Jr. He gave a speech at a community meeting that same night. He said, "One of the great glories of democracy is the right to protest for right." Moved by his words, everyone decided to extend the boycott.

The boycott lasted for over a year. Finally, on November 13, 1956, the U.S. Supreme Court outlawed bus segregation. On December 21, blacks once again rode Montgomery's buses.

....

Number the events in correct time order.

_____ E. D. Nixon calls Reverend Ralph Abernathy.

_____ Rosa Parks is arrested.

_____ Sign is posted at the bus stop announcing the boycott.

_____ Supreme Court outlaws bus segregation.

_____ Rosa Parks refuses to give up her seat to a white man.

_____ Martin Luther King, Jr., becomes the leader of the protest.

Check your answers on page 157.

WRITING WORKSHOP

Brainstorm: Make a List

In this chapter, you read about some events in American history. What are the major events that make up your personal history? Make a list of the events in your life and the dates they occurred. For example, your list might include your birthday, your graduation date, your wedding date, or other special moments.

Focus: Create a Time Line

Review your list, and choose five of the most important events. Then create a time line to summarize these events. Use the time lines on page 27 as a model.

Expand: Write a Paragraph

Describe your time line in a paragraph. Add some details about the events in your time line. Use time order to organize the information in your paragraph.

CHAPTER 5 | CAUSE AND EFFECT

Picture the details described in this weather report:

> A blizzard struck the Midwest today. Temperatures dipped below zero. High winds and heavy snowfall have made traveling dangerous. Many airports have shut down and canceled flights. The list of school closings continues to grow.

The details in the weather report are arranged in a pattern called **cause and effect**. The weather report tells you what happened—a blizzard. It also explains the results of the blizzard: airports shut down and schools closed.

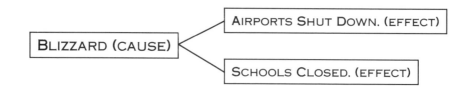

■ Analyze the cause-and-effect relationships of these two statements.

▶ Because of the thunderstorms, the electricity went out.

▶ The streets were icy, so cars were skidding.

The clue words *because* and *so* signal what happened and why.

Did you know that weather also has influenced the course of American history? As you read the following passage, think about how one event led to another event.

The Dust Bowl

> 'Long about nineteen thirty-one,
> My field burnt up in the boiling sun.
> 'Long about nineteen thirty-two,
> Dust did rise and the dust it blew. ©

These lines from Woody Guthrie's song "End of My Line" describe a farming disaster in the 1930s. The disaster occurred in an area from North Dakota to Texas, spanning about 50 million acres. This area became known as the "Dust Bowl."

The problems began in the early 1930s. Overgrazing and poor land management were ruining the topsoil. A severe drought caused the land to dry out, and the topsoil began to blow away. This caused terrible dust storms that darkened the skies for thousands of miles. The crops dried up. Thousands of families were forced to give up their land and leave their homes. Most families headed for

California hoping to find jobs. These people were called "Okies," although they didn't all come from Oklahoma. John Steinbeck's famous book *The Grapes of Wrath* is about the Okies who went west.

By the early 1940s, the problems were almost resolved. The drought finally ended, and the federal government helped to restore the land.

· ·

Let's look more closely at how the passage is organized. The topic of the passage is the Dust Bowl. The writer arranges the details in time order to explain the sequence of events. He also analyzes the causes and effects within that sequence.

▪ Can you find which events are causes and which are effects? Next to each statement below, write the word *cause* or *effect*.

_____ Farming methods damaged the soil.

_____ Windstorms swept away topsoil.

_____ Farms were turned into deserts.

_____ Farm families left their farms and went west.

The first two statements explain causes. They answer the question: Why did the Dust Bowl occur? The last two statements explain effects. They answer the question: What were the results of the Dust Bowl?

STRATEGY: HOW TO UNDERSTAND CAUSE AND EFFECT

▶ Pay close attention to the sequence of events.
▶ Notice if one event caused another event to occur. What happened? Why?
▶ Look for the clue words: *because, as a result, so, therefore,* and *since.*
▶ Check the topic sentences to see if they state the cause-and-effect relationships detailed in the passage.

Exercise 1

Read the passage and complete the exercise that follows.

Why do people join labor unions? Do you think labor unions help protect workers?

The Rise of Labor Unions

With the growth of industry and factories in the late 1800s, working conditions worsened in the United States. Most of the factory workers then were immigrants who came from Europe. In 1905, an average workweek was 58 hours. An average weekly pay was only $25. The situation was even worse for women and blacks. By 1906, more than 60% of American workers were unable to earn enough money to support a family.

The work was usually boring and the conditions were often dangerous. Many people worked in "sweatshops." These were places where people worked and sometimes lived. They were usually dirty, unsafe, and overcrowded.

Many children also worked in the factories and sweatshops. In the early 1900s, almost two million children were working. In the South, about one-third of all cotton mill workers were children. Many families were unable to send their children to school.

Workers were unhappy with the working conditions and, as a result, Labor unions began to grow. Unions fought to solve the workers' problems. They wanted the owners to increase wages and decrease the number of hours people had to work. They also fought to end child labor. The owners did not want the workers to join the unions. Conflicts arose between the two groups. In the United States, it wasn't until the 1930s that workers were finally granted the legal right to join unions.

PART A

Circle the best answer for each question.

1. What angered the workers?
   (1) too many European immigrants
   (2) poverty and terrible working conditions
   (3) police involved in labor conflicts
   (4) American cities

2. What is the topic sentence of the last paragraph?
   (1) Workers were unhappy with the working conditions, and, as a result, labor unions began to grow.
   (2) These groups fought to improve American workers' lives.
   (3) Unions wanted to outlaw child labor.
   (4) They wanted to increase hourly pay.

3. According to the passage, what happened when labor unions demanded better working conditions?
   (1) Cruel employers said that workers were like machines.
   (2) Employers started treating workers fairly.
   (3) Workers became happy, healthy employees.
   (4) Conflicts often broke out between owners and workers.

PART B

Answer the questions in the space provided.

1. How much might a man earn for a fourteen-hour workday in the late 1800s?

   _____

2. List three conditions that made sweatshops so bad in the early 1900s.

   (a) _____

   (b) _____

   (c) _____

Check your answers on page 157.

Exercise 2

Read the passage and complete the exercises that follow.

The Wild West is a period of American history dating from 1865 to 1900. What are your views of this time, based on Hollywood westerns? Why do you think there were so many outlaws during the Wild West period?

The Wild West

John Wesley Hardin was a preacher's son with a bad temper: "They tell a lot of lies about me. They say I killed six or seven men for snoring, but it isn't true. I only killed one man for snoring." This famous outlaw from Texas admitted to killing 44 people.

The terror of Jesse James and his gang remains a legend in American history. Bank holdups, train robberies, and killings were their stock and trade. Butch Cassidy and his band, the Wild Bunch, earned their fame as train robbers. Posters offered rewards for killers, outlaws, and crooks. These criminals were products of the Wild West.

Why was the West so wild? After the Civil War ended in 1865, many Southerners were bitter. Some held grudges against the North. John Wesley Hardin said that his life was a "flight not from justice, but from the injustice . . . of the people who had **subjugated**[1] the South." As a young **Confederate**[2] soldier, Jesse James fought in bloody battles. He never lost his taste for violence and killing.

During the 1880s, terrible weather and a depression in the cattle country spelled disaster for cowboys. As a result, many cowboys were out of work. Some, like the Wild Bunch, turned to a life of crime.

The lack of law officers and jails also made the West wild. Many men cared more about staying alive than wearing a sheriff's badge. Some people carried out their own brand of justice. They held "necktie parties," where they hanged the outlaws they caught.

---

[1]subjugated: brought under control
[2]Confederate: one who fought for the South in the Civil War

PART A

Write *cause* or *effect* on the lines.

1. _____ Because they lost the Civil War,

   _____ many Southerners felt bitter toward the North.

2. _____ Jesse James fought in the Civil War;

   _____ therefore, he knew about violence and killing.

3. _____ Many cowboys were out of work and turned to crime

   _____ as a result of terrible weather and a depression in the 1880s.

4. _____ Since there were not enough law officers and jails in the
   Wild West,

   _____ some citizens held "necktie parties," where they hanged
   outlaws.

5. _____ John Wesley Hardin killed a man for snoring

   _____ because he had a violent temper.

PART B

Circle the best answer for each question.

1. What is the main idea of the passage?
   - **(1)** how terrible weather spelled disaster for cowboys
   - **(2)** how the Wild Bunch earned its fame
   - **(3)** why the West was so wild
   - **(4)** why "necktie" parties were held

2. Why was Jesse James so violent?
   - **(1)** He liked to hold up banks and rob trains.
   - **(2)** A depression in the cattle country made him angry.
   - **(3)** He was a product of the Wild West.
   - **(4)** He got a taste for killing as a soldier in the Civil War.

Check your answers on page 157.

Exercise 3

Read the passage and complete the exercises that follow.

Do you depend on a car for transportation? How has the automobile influenced American life?

How the Car Changed America

During the 1920s, American society began to feel the effects of the car. New factories and suburbs sprang up in areas that were once wilderness. Main streets became dotted with traffic signals. Gas stations and hot dog stands opened. By the end of the 1920s, there were also motels and many billboards.

More roads connected the city and the country. Farmers began driving regularly into cities and towns. City people rode miles into the country for picnics. The romance of the road lured millions to take long car trips. Many followed the popular slogan "See America First." They drove to tourist spots from Florida to California.

The growth of the car industry had its bad effects, too. The number of car accidents soared. Traffic jams, street noise, and smoke often caused major problems. Some parents blamed cars for encouraging teenagers to have sex. Without their parents, they went on dates in closed cars. Criminals could use "getaway" cars to escape the police.

Will Rogers once made this comment about Henry Ford: "It will take a hundred years to tell whether you have helped us or hurt us, but you certainly didn't leave us like you found us." This comment also applies to the car industry during the late 1920s.

PART A
Circle the best answer for each question.

1. The main purpose of the passage is to
   (1) trace the growth of the car industry
   (2) explain teenagers' behavior
   (3) show the effects of cars during the 1920s
   (4) explain the causes of car accidents and traffic jams

2. Farmers began driving regularly into cities because of the
- **(1)** new suburbs
- **(2)** increase in roads
- **(3)** gas stations and hot dog stands
- **(4)** tourist spots

3. Which statement describes a bad effect of the car?
- **(1)** Main streets became dotted with traffic signals.
- **(2)** People drove long distances to see America.
- **(3)** Factories were built in the wilderness.
- **(4)** Criminals used cars to escape the police.

PART B

List two good effects and two bad effects of cars in the 1920s.

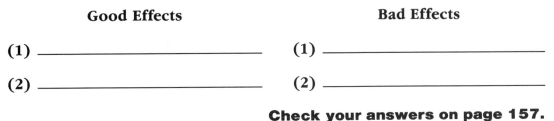

Good Effects	Bad Effects
(1) _____	**(1)** _____
(2) _____	**(2)** _____

Check your answers on page 157.

WRITING WORKSHOP

Brainstorm: Make a List

In this chapter, you read how the car affected American society in the 1920s. Write a list of machines or inventions that have a good effect on your life. Think of machines you use at home or at your job, such as the telephone or computer.

Focus: Write a Topic Sentence

Choose a machine from your list to write about. Write a topic sentence in the form of a question: What would happen if ____ had never been invented?

Expand: Write a Paragraph

Answer your topic sentence in a paragraph. Write the results of living without the machine. Remember, all the sentences in your paragraph should explain effects.

CHAPTER 6 | PROBLEM AND SOLUTION

Every day, people write letters to the newspapers about their personal problems. The beginning of each letter usually describes the situation that is causing the problem. Then the writer expects answers to these basic questions:

▶ What should I do?

▶ What are my choices?

▶ What course of action should I take to change or improve the situation?

In response, the advice columnist offers a solution. This approach to analyzing a situation is called **problem and solution**.

Similarly, the details in many social studies passages are also arranged in a problem-and-solution pattern. In the following passage, find out how an American citizen from the 1800s reacted to a problem. Then answer the questions about the passage.

Civil Disobedience

Henry David Thoreau

In 1846, the United States declared war on Mexico. Henry David Thoreau was against the war. He felt its goal was to increase slave territory. "Unjust laws exist," he wrote, "but shall we obey them?" Thoreau believed that the answer was to "resist" the American government, "which is the *slave's* government also." In protest, he refused to pay his **poll tax**[1] to Massachusetts. As a result, he was thrown into jail. Thoreau made this comment about prison: It is "the only house in a slave State in which a free man can abide with Honor."

Thoreau's essay "Civil Disobedience" offered solutions for the problem of injustice. He believed that people had the right to rebel against laws they thought were wrong. Thoreau favored nonviolent protest. His ideas inspired Martin Luther King, Jr. King believed in Thoreau's solutions. King organized marches and other nonviolent protests. These were King's weapons for attacking racial injustice.

---

¹poll tax: a fee people had to pay before they could vote

■ Answer the questions in the space provided.

In "Civil Disobedience," what problem did Thoreau discuss?

_____

According to Thoreau, what right did people have to solve this problem?

_____

Thoreau's essay discussed the problem of injustice. He felt that people had the right to rebel against laws that they firmly believed were wrong.

Causes and effects are often included in social studies passages that discuss a problem and solution. An event may create a problem. For example, the war against Mexico caused Thoreau to face the problem of slavery.

In turn, solutions to problems can have lasting effects. Thoreau's "Civil Disobedience" affected how Martin Luther King, Jr., protested unjust laws in the United States and how Gandhi protested Britain's control of India.

STRATEGY: HOW TO UNDERSTAND PROBLEM AND SOLUTION

▶ Identify the problem that is facing a person, group, or nation.
▶ Find a solution. What course of action is taken to improve the situation?
▶ Look for causes and effects. Why did the problem arise? What were the results of the solution?
▶ Check to see if the solution was successful.

Exercise 1

Read the passage and complete the exercise that follows.

Should laws control people's personal habits? How would you react if a law was passed today forbidding alcohol?

Prohibition

Nowadays, "the night belongs to Michelob." Sports fans hold cans of beer and chant, "Less filling! Tastes great!" Budweiser beer cans use the colors of the American flag. Attempts to limit beer sales at ball games are shot down. In light of this, can you believe that America once outlawed alcohol?

America has often tried seemingly simple solutions to tough problems. Indians on good land? Move them out. Crime a problem? Bring back the death penalty. These easy solutions rarely work the way they are supposed to.

How should the country solve the social problems caused by drinking? America attempted another simple solution. It, too, was a huge failure. In 1919, Congress passed the Eighteenth **Amendment**[1] of the **Constitution**.[2] It **prohibited**[3] making, selling, and moving liquors within the United States. National prohibition went into effect in 1920.

President Herbert Hoover believed in Prohibition. It was "a great social and economic experiment, noble in motive." But author Mark Twain didn't agree. To him, this law "drove drunkenness behind doors into dark places and [did] not cure . . . it."

---

[1]**Amendment:** a change in wording or meaning in a law
[2]**Constitution:** the basic beliefs and laws of a nation that establish the powers and duties of the government and guarantee certain rights to the people
[3]**prohibited:** made illegal

Mark Twain was right. Instead of solving problems, Prohibition created new ones. For example, Prohibition was hard to enforce and helped organized crime grow. Gangsters smuggled and sold illegal liquor. They met the needs of ordinary people who still wanted to drink, despite the law.

Adapted from *Don't Know Much About History*, by Kenneth C. Davis

Circle the best answer for each question.

1. In 1919, what problem did the government try to solve?
   (1) beer commercials
   (2) crime
   (3) social problems caused by drinking
   (4) Indians

2. What was Congress's solution to the main problem discussed in the passage?
   (1) enforcing the death penalty
   (2) passing the Eighteenth Amendment
   (3) removing Indians from their land
   (4) banning liquor at ball games

3. What was one effect of Prohibition?
   (1) It was a noble cause that had economic benefits.
   (2) It solved the social problems caused by drinking.
   (3) It met the needs of ordinary people.
   (4) It helped organized crime increase.

4. What point does the author of the passage make about problem solving?
   (1) Simple solutions to tough problems rarely work the way they are supposed to.
   (2) Social problems, such as crime, are the easiest to solve.
   (3) Problem solving is a social experiment.
   (4) Grand attempts to solve problems always lead to big failures.

Check your answers on page 157.

Exercise 2

Read the passage and complete the exercise that follows.

How would you feel if you were forced to move out of your home and your neighborhood? Why were the Cherokee Indians forced to leave their homes?

The Trail of Tears

In the early 1800s, cotton was "king" in the South. Some Native American tribes lived in the southeastern United States. But they got in the way of "King Cotton." They were on valuable land for growing this all-important crop. Georgia was the cotton-growing state where most Cherokee Indians lived. Georgia pressured the U.S. government to force the Cherokees to leave.

Bowing to this pressure, Congress took action. It passed the Indian Removal Act in 1830. According to this law, Native Americans would give up their land. In exchange, they would settle in new territories west of the Mississippi River. President Jackson thought this was a fair solution to a tough problem. He said, "This unhappy race are now placed in a situation where we may well hope that they will share in the blessings of civilization. . . ."

To the Cherokees in Georgia, the Indian Removal Act was not a blessing. Instead, it was a curse. They refused to leave their homeland. In 1838, President Van Buren enforced the policy of removal. Federal troops rounded up over 17,000 Cherokees in Georgia. They marched the Cherokees to Arkansas.

John G. Burnett, an army private, described the journey: "I saw the helpless Cherokees arrested and dragged from their homes. . . . I saw them loaded like cattle or sheep into 645 wagons and headed for the West. . . . The trail of the **exiles**[1] was a trail of death." About 4,000 died along the way. This forced march became known as "The Trail of Tears."

Ralph Waldo Emerson, a writer, was shocked by this cruel episode in American history. He wrote, "Such a denial of justice, and such deafness to screams for mercy were never heard . . . since the earth was made."

. . . .

Answer the questions in the space provided.

1. Before the Civil War, what was the most valuable crop in the South?

_____

2. Why did Georgia want the Cherokees to leave the state?

_____

_____

3. What was the Indian Removal Act?

_____

_____

4. What was President Jackson's opinion of the Indian Removal Act?

_____

_____

5. How did the Cherokees respond to the Indian Removal Act?

_____

6. What was the "Trail of Tears"?

_____

_____

Check your answers on pages 157-158.

_____

¹exiles: people driven from their homes

Exercise 3

Read the passage and complete the exercise that follows.

What would you do if banks weren't safe places to keep money? How do people react when they lose faith in the government?

President Roosevelt Tackles a Problem

Franklin D. Roosevelt

The Great Depression of the 1930s brought unemployment and suffering. The economy plunged and feelings of panic and fear soared. Americans' faith in the government was shaken. Franklin Roosevelt became president in 1933 with hopes to boost the economy. He also wanted to raise people's spirits. In his first **inaugural address**,[1] he made this famous statement: "The only thing we have to fear is fear itself. . . ."

Out of fear, people were rushing to their banks to withdraw their money. The first crisis facing Roosevelt was solving the banking problem. Two days after his inauguration, Roosevelt declared a "bank holiday." The government closed all the banks in the country for four days. Congress then passed the Emergency Banking Act. It gave the government the power to inspect banking methods and records. To reopen, banks had to meet the government's standards.

Next, Roosevelt held his first "fireside chat." He spoke to people over the radio. "My friends, I want to talk a few minutes to the people of the United States about banking. . . . I want to tell you what has been done in the last few days, why it was done, and what the next steps are going to be." He asked everyone to trust the banking system: "It is safer to keep your money in a reopened bank than it is under the mattress." Roosevelt's radio talk drove away the public's fears. People flocked to the banks to deposit their savings.

Roosevelt's regular radio talks made Americans feel better. They felt that they were working with Roosevelt. They felt that together they were solving the huge problems of the Great Depression. Roosevelt himself said that his solutions might not always work. He practiced this approach to problem solving: "Take a method and try it. If it fails, admit it frankly and try another."

---

[1]inaugural address: speech a president makes when sworn into office

Circle *T* for true or *F* for false.

T   F   **1.** The Great Depression caused suffering, panic, and fear.

T   F   **2.** The first problem Roosevelt solved was unemployment.

T   F   **3.** During the "bank holiday," people rushed to the banks to withdraw their savings.

T   F   **4.** Congress passed the Emergency Banking Act to help solve the nation's banking problem.

T   F   **5.** During his first fireside chat, Roosevelt explained his actions, the reasons for his actions, and his future plans.

T   F   **6.** When the banks reopened, people decided to keep their money under their mattresses.

T   F   **7.** Roosevelt was sure that his solutions to problems would always be successful.

Check your answers on page 158.

WRITING WORKSHOP

Brainstorm: Make a List

In this chapter, you read about President Roosevelt's fireside chats. Because of these radio talks, people felt they could confide in him. While Roosevelt was president, many Americans wrote him letters. Make a list of problems you think the current president should try to solve.

Focus: Identify the Problem

From your list, choose a few of the most serious problems. For example, your list might include unemployment, crime, drugs, homelessness, the economy, education, or tax rates.

Expand: Write a Letter

Write a letter to the president. Give some background information about the problems you think need to be solved. End your letter by suggesting some solutions that the president should think about.

CHAPTER 7 | COMPARISON AND CONTRAST

> Dare to compare! Take a test drive in our Cruiser van. Compare comfort and performance. Compare price. Then shop around. You'll see that our Cruiser van beats all other vans.

This ad tells you to decide if the Cruiser is the same as other vans. When you **compare** things, you find out how they are alike. When you **contrast** things, you find out how they are different. This approach is called **comparison and contrast**.

Many social studies passages show a comparison and contrast. They tell how people, situations, or ideas are similar and different. Sometimes a comparison and contrast shows a change.

■ Learn what family life was like *before* and *after* the Civil War. Read the following passage. Underline the clue words that show comparison and contrast.

The Father's Changing Role

On the farms and in small towns, fathers worked near their families. Before the **Civil War**[1] (1860–1865), even city workers had jobs close to their homes. Most families were centered around the father and the home.

However, in the late 1800s, cities grew. This changed the family. The father's role also changed. Working-class men who could afford it rode streetcars to work. They took jobs farther away from their homes. Thus, they spent much more time away from their families.

Before the Civil War, the father's world was still tied to his family. But now the worlds within the family grew apart. The shop, office, and factory were for men. In contrast, the home and school were for women and children.

The father's absence from home caused problems for his children. For example, sons missed their fathers. In the past, fathers and sons had been closer. Sons felt lost without their fathers. Young men found adjusting to work harder, and becoming an adult was more difficult.

---

[1]**Civil War:** a war between the U.S. federal government and eleven southern states that wanted to separate from the Union

Did you underline the clue words **however** and **in contrast**? These words signal differences. The growth of cities after the Civil War made the father's role different.

The passage shows two contrasting pictures of the father. First, imagine a father spending most of his time with his family at home. Then, imagine a father spending most of his time at his job.

▨ Where did men, women, and children spend most of their time? Use the passage to fill in the lines.

men _____ _____ _____

women and children _____ _____

Here are the answers: **men—shop, office, factory; women and children— school, home.**

STRATEGY: HOW TO UNDERSTAND COMPARISON AND CONTRAST

▸ Find the topic. What people, ideas, or situations are compared or contrasted?

▸ Search for details that explain the topic. What is alike? What is different?

▸ Look for clue words that signal comparison and contrast. Examples include *like, similarly, in contrast, instead,* and *however.*

Exercise 1

Read the passage and complete the exercise that follows.

Why did the role of women change from World War II to the 1950s?
How are women portrayed today on TV and in ads?

Rosie the Riveter and June Cleaver

She rolled up her sleeves and wore overalls. She carried a lunch bucket under her arm. She punched a time clock in a factory. She built war planes, ships, and army tanks. A national heroine was born. Her name was "Rosie the Riveter."

This character appeared on posters and magazine covers. She called on American women to serve their country during **World War II**.[1] Women took the challenge. They worked in defense plants across the country. Meanwhile, millions of men fought overseas.

In the 1940s, Rosie the Riveter represented women's role during a war. However, after the war, the image of Rosie the Riveter quickly faded. Her work clothes were no longer in style. Her job skills were no longer needed. Women factory workers were fired. Men returning from the war were hired to fill those jobs. A woman's place, once again, was in the home.

In the 1950s, Rosie the Riveter was replaced with other role models. TV characters became the new ideal. June Cleaver, the mother in "Leave It to Beaver," seemed perfect. Unlike Rosie the Riveter, June Cleaver wore dresses. She often wore pearls and high heels. She didn't weld or rivet. Instead, June Cleaver cleaned the house. Her job was to stay at home and be a mother and wife. Most ads showed women like June Cleaver. They were happy housewives using the latest kitchen products.

These two contrasting images show how history shaped the idealized roles of American women. During wartime, Rosie the Riveter worked to preserve freedom. During peacetime, June Cleaver worked to preserve family life.

---

[1]**World War II:** a conflict fought between the Axis Powers—Germany, Italy, and Japan—and the Allies—primarily France, Great Britain, the United States, the Soviet Union, and China—from 1939 to 1945

Rosie the Riveter

1950s Housewife

Fill in the chart in the spaces provided.

	Rosie the Riveter	**June Cleaver**
1. When was each woman popular?		
2. What did each woman wear?		
3. What was each woman's job?		
4. Where did each woman work?		
5. What was each woman's purpose?		

Check your answers on page 158.

Exercise 2

Read the passage and complete the exercise that follows.

What makes a political leader popular? Would President Lincoln win an election if he were alive today?

A Lesson from Lincoln's Life

What was in **Abraham Lincoln**'s[1] pockets on the night he died? The **Library of Congress**[2] stores these items from Lincoln's life. He had a pair of glasses, some money, and a pocket knife. The knife may have dated back to his days on the prairie.

A news story about Lincoln was also in his pocket. The article, written during that last year of the Civil War, gave Lincoln a small amount of praise for the job he was doing. Lincoln did not get very much public praise for his handling of the war.

Unlike most modern presidents, Lincoln listened to Americans. As president, he was under great pressure. Yet he talked to mothers whose sons were missing because of the war. He gave advice to wives whose husbands were in prison.

These meetings were demanding. For strength, Lincoln read the Bible each night. The verses reminded him that true wisdom "comes from God and not from man."

Lincoln might not be accepted as a leader today. He talked about the God who gave him moral strength. He was not a handsome man. He also refrained from criticizing those who opposed him. In contrast, today's political **candidates**[3] place more importance on style than on **moral values**.[4] Presenting a smooth image on TV wins votes. Also, criticizing opponents is common during political campaigns.

Today's leaders could learn a lesson from Lincoln. He defended his beliefs as president. He paid little attention to others' praise or criticism. Lincoln found that his strength came from the faith and moral values within himself.

---

[1] **Abraham Lincoln:** 16th president of the United States
[2] **Library of Congress:** the national library of the United States, founded in Washington, D.C., in 1800
[3] **candidate:** one who runs in an election
[4] **moral values:** beliefs about what is right and wrong

PART A

Circle *T* for true or *F* for false.

T   F   **1.** The article criticized Lincoln's handling of the war.

T   F   **2.** According to the passage, Lincoln would probably be accepted as a leader today.

T   F   **3.** According to the passage, unlike Lincoln, today's political candidates emphasize style more than moral values.

T   F   **4.** Lincoln found strength by reading the Bible instead of newspapers.

T   F   **5.** According to the passage, today's leaders could learn a lesson from Lincoln and try to be more like him.

PART B

Circle the best answer for the question.

The main idea of the cartoon is that
(a) Lincoln was a loser.
(b) Lincoln went to an image specialist.
(c) Lincoln might not be elected today if he were running for president.
(d) No bearded man has ever been elected president.

Check your answers on page 158.

Exercise 3

Read the passage and complete the exercise that follows.

What is more important—economic success or political freedom? How did two African-American leaders value these goals?

Booker T. Washington and W. E. B. DuBois

Booker T. Washington

W. E. B. DuBois

Both Booker T. Washington and W. E. B. DuBois wanted to improve the lives of African Americans. They strongly agreed on this goal. Yet they disagreed on the way to achieve it.

In 1895, Booker T. Washington gave a famous speech. He described the path that African Americans should follow: "No race can prosper till it learns that there is as much dignity in tilling a field as in writing a poem. It is at the bottom of life we must begin, and not at the top." Washington preached the value of hard work. He urged African Americans to get job training. As a result, they could improve their economic rank in society. Gaining political and social equality was not the chief aim.

However, W. E. B. DuBois felt that Washington aimed too low. In 1903, DuBois wrote an essay responding to Washington's ideas. To DuBois, Washington's "gospel of Work and Money" seemed "almost completely to **overshadow**[1] the higher aims of life." DuBois, like Washington, thought that economic growth was important. But DuBois believed that **segregation**[2] blocked economic growth.

Unlike Washington, DuBois thought African Americans should fight for their civil rights. He said that it was segregation that blocked their climb toward success. DuBois felt that Washington stressed pleasing whites and this meant accepting unfair laws.

---

[1]**overshadow:** to become more important than
[2]**segregation:** racial, political, and social separation of people

Circle the best answer for each question.

1. What issue did both Washington and DuBois address?

  (1) teaching people to write poetry

  (2) making life better for African Americans

  (3) training people for jobs

  (4) tilling the fields

2. What goal did both Washington and DuBois think was important?

  (1) achieving economic growth

  (2) ending segregation

  (3) getting along with white people

  (4) accepting unfair laws

3. How did DuBois's views differ from Washington's?

  (1) DuBois thought earning money wasn't necessary.

  (2) DuBois felt reaching economic goals didn't matter.

  (3) DuBois believed that fighting for civil rights should be a primary goal.

  (4) DuBois thought jobs were more important than politics.

Check your answers on page 158.

WRITING WORKSHOP

Brainstorm: Write a List

In this chapter, you read about Rosie the Riveter from the 1940s and June Cleaver from the 1950s. Think of two women characters from TV shows of the 1990s. Examples include Clair Huxtable (of "The Cosby Show"), Roseanne Conner (of "Roseanne"), and Murphy Brown. Write a list describing how the women are alike and how they are different. You might compare and contrast their appearances, jobs, and family lives.

Focus: Make a Chart

Make a comparison-and-contrast chart similar to the one on page 51. At the top of the chart, write each woman's name. Complete the chart with the information from your list.

Expand: Write a Paragraph

Write a paragraph that provides background information about your chart. For instance, you might write a brief summary of the TV shows in which these characters appear.

UNIT 2
REVIEW

Read the passage and complete the exercise that follows.

Have you ever read a book that greatly influenced you? Can written words change the course of history?

The Power of Writing

A scene from *Uncle Tom's Cabin*

The TV series *Roots* showed Americans the pain of slavery. Harriet Beecher Stowe's novel *Uncle Tom's Cabin* did the same for 19th-century Americans. In the 18th century, Thomas Paine's pamphlet *Common Sense* swayed American colonists. It convinced them to rebel against British rule.

Paine and Stowe both had strong beliefs. Paine, an American colonist, was born in England. He hated his homeland's type of government. The king had complete power and ruled over his subjects. Stowe was born in New England. She opposed slavery for religious reasons.

Paine arrived in America in 1774. In January 1776, he published *Common Sense*. He called King George III "the royal brute." Paine attacked the evils of the British government. He contrasted it with a true democracy. He compared colonists to grown-up children: They were now strong enough to break ties with their parent country, England. They were ready to survive alone.

Within six months, *Common Sense* sold over 150,000 copies. No colonist could ignore its ideas about independence. It gave people faith in themselves. They believed they could create, organize, and run a democracy.

Similarly, Stowe's *Uncle Tom's Cabin* stirred the nation to support another great cause. In 1850, the Fugitive Slave Law was passed. It helped slave owners capture their runaway slaves. This law angered Stowe. She vowed to show the whole nation the horrors of slavery. This was the purpose of her novel.

Published in 1852, *Uncle Tom's Cabin* shocked the North. It sold 300,000 copies the first year. During the next ten years, it sold over 2 million more copies. In the South, slave owners tried to ban the book. Also, at least fifteen novels in favor of slavery were written. However, none could stop the political effect of Stowe's book. Later, President Lincoln met Stowe. He supposedly said, "So you're the little woman who wrote the book that made this great war [the Civil War]."

Adapted from *Independence and Abolitionism*, by Jim Podesta

Circle the best answer for each question.

1. How were Thomas Paine and Harriet Beecher Stowe alike?
   (1) They both wrote powerful novels.
   (2) They both shared strong beliefs.
   (3) They were both born in England.
   (4) They both opposed the government for religious reasons.

2. What happened in 1774 and then in January 1776?
   (1) Thomas Paine arrived in America and then published *Common Sense*.
   (2) George III became the king of England and then was called a "royal brute."
   (3) Thomas Paine published *Common Sense* and then moved to America.
   (4) *Common Sense* sold over 150,000 copies and then Stowe wrote *Uncle Tom's Cabin*.

3. What problem was the Fugitive Slave Law supposed to solve?
   (1) the problem of cruel slave owners
   (2) the problem of runaway slaves
   (3) the horrors of slavery
   (4) the conflict between the North and South

4. President Lincoln supposedly told Stowe that he thought she was responsible for causing
   (1) the Fugitive Slave Law
   (2) an increase in book sales
   (3) a ban on novels
   (4) the Civil War

Check your answers on page 158.

UNIT 3
POLITICAL SCIENCE

How do governments work? What laws guide people's actions? How do nations around the world get along with one another? Political scientists search for the answers to these questions. Political scientists and historians explore some of the same issues. Both study governments, laws, and war. **Political science** focuses on the ideas, problems, and behavior of governments.

POLITICAL SCIENCE
TOPICS

- Facts About Handguns
- The Birth of a Government
- The Death of the Soviet Union
- Should People Sue So Much?
- Vietnam Veterans Come Home
- What Is a Democrat?
- Privacy Ends at Work
- UNICEF Cares for the World's Children
- Women's Future in Politics
- The Threat of Nuclear Weapons
- A Victory for Women Athletes
- Modern Campaigns for President
- Political Parties and the Economy
- The Politics of Health Care
- The Business Side of War
- Equal Opportunity?
- The Threat of Terrorism

AFTER READING THIS UNIT, YOU SHOULD BE ABLE TO

▶ FIND FACTS AND OPINIONS
▶ MAKE INFERENCES
▶ PREDICT OUTCOMES
▶ UNDERSTAND POLITICAL CARTOONS

CHAPTER 8 | FACT AND OPINION

On a job application, you write facts about yourself:

- Your name, address, and phone number
- Your birth date and social security number
- Your work experience
- Your education

On many job applications you are asked to sign your name to a statement similar to the following:

> I confirm that all the information in this application is
> true. I understand that if I give false information I may
> lose my job.

In other words, job applications must have only facts. A **fact** is a statement that can be proved true.

An **opinion** is a statement that tells someone's feelings or beliefs. You may agree or disagree with someone's opinion. During a job interview, you might explain why you should be hired:

- "I think I get along well with people."
- "I feel that I learn quickly."

The words *I think* and *I feel* are clues that these statements are opinions.

Many social studies passages contain both facts and opinions. Writers often use facts to support their opinions. As you read the following "Letter to the Editor," look for facts and opinions.

Handgun Facts

I want to answer the June 8 letter titled "Self-Defense Guns," by Max Harper. The letter didn't present a true picture.

These are the cold, hard facts:

- Handguns kill more than 1,000 children each year. They injure thousands more.
- There are over 60 million registered handguns in the United States.
- The United States has the most handgun killings in the world.

We are killing ourselves, and for what? Did you know that more than 1 million legally owned guns are used by law-abiding citizens? You stand a better chance of being killed by someone you know than by a criminal.

Education is important. We need to learn more about safety. We also need to change our attitudes. Owning and using handguns doesn't solve problems.

We must find a better way. Until we do, we will keep killing each other at alarmingly higher and higher rates. One day this may change.

. . . .

■ Read the following sentences. Then circle *F* if the statement is a fact or *O* if it is an opinion.

F O **1.** Over 60 million handguns are registered in the United States.

F O **2.** Many steps must be taken to stop handgun killings.

F O **3.** People need to change their attitudes about handguns.

F O **4.** The United States ranks first in the world in handgun killings.

F O **5.** More than 1 million legally owned guns are used by law-abiding citizens.

F O **6.** You stand a better chance of being killed by someone you know than by a criminal.

Here are the answers: 1. **F**, 2. **O**, 3. **O**, 4. **F**, 5. **F**, 6. **F**

Did you notice that the writer begins the letter with facts? These facts shape his opinion.

STRATEGY: HOW TO IDENTIFY FACTS AND OPINIONS

▶ Find the information that can be proved true.
▶ Look for clue words that signal opinions. Examples include *I believe, I feel, I think,* and *in my opinion.*
▶ Check to be sure that the opinions are supported by the facts.

Exercise 1

Read the passage and complete the exercise that follows.

What are the problems of building a government? What are the beliefs that built American government?

The Birth of a Government

Suppose you had to build a government. How would you begin? Would you just pick a leader? Would you then let the leader choose the way to build a government? Or would you just set up a few rules, hoping they might work?

By 1787, many Americans knew that the United States needed a new government. They chose a group to build a new government for them. This group met in Philadelphia. Today we call this meeting the Constitutional Convention.

The members of the Convention were lucky. They had help from the past in solving their problems. In early times, people had discovered certain rules of political science. These rules helped them to form strong governments. Two ideas were very important. One came from the Greek city-state of Athens. The other came from Rome.

The Greek idea was democracy. In fact, the word *democracy* comes from the Greek language. It means "rule of the people." In a democracy, the people themselves are the government. The people choose their own laws and leaders. They can decide what the government should do. The idea of democracy is similar to the idea of popular consent. This means that the people consent, or agree, to follow certain laws and leaders.

The Convention wanted the people to rule. Yet they wanted to make sure that the people would be fair. So they turned to another idea. This idea came from the Romans. It was the rule of law. The Romans believed that there must be a written law and that this written law must be the same for all people. One group could not change the law to suit itself. Even the government must obey the law!

The Convention put the Greek idea and the Roman idea together. The result was a form of government called constitutional democracy.

Adapted from *Greek and Roman Civilization*,
by the Educational Research Council of America

First Constitutional Convention in Philadephia in 1787

PART A

Circle *F* for a fact or *O* for an opinion.

F O **1.** In 1787, the Constitutional Convention met in Philadelphia.

F O **2.** Greeks and Romans had mostly good ideas.

F O **3.** *Democracy*, a Greek word, means "rule of the people."

F O **4.** Democracy is the best form of government.

F O **5.** Popular consent means that people agree to follow certain laws and leaders.

F O **6.** The idea of a written law comes from the Romans.

F O **7.** Laws should treat people fairly.

PART B

According to the passage, which statements are true in a democracy? You may check (✓) more than one.

____ **(1)** The government sets up the rules and hopes they will work.
____ **(2)** A leader chooses the way to build a government.
____ **(3)** The people choose their own laws and leaders.
____ **(4)** One group can change the law to suit itself.
____ **(5)** The people decide what the government should do.

Check your answers on pages 158-159.

Exercise 2

Read the passage and complete the exercise that follows.

What forms of government do you know about besides democracy?
Why do some governments fail?

The Death of the Soviet Union

Karl Marx

Karl Marx (1818–1883) lived in an age of dirty factories filled with smoke. During this time, factory owners hired children. People worked six days a week. There was also great poverty.

These problems angered Marx. He felt they would only get worse. He thought the rich would get richer. Meanwhile, the poor would get poorer. Conditions would become so bad, Marx believed, that workers would rebel. They would then set up a communist system. In this system, everyone would share the wealth equally. Many people followed Marx's ideas. They called themselves Marxists, or communists.

In 1917, a Russian named Vladimir Lenin and his followers set up the first communist government. In 1922 the Soviet Union was founded. The Soviet Union was made up of republics. Communist ideals united them.

But, instead of freedom, the Soviet people got a brutal dictatorship. Instead of happiness, they suffered hardship and death. Instead of peace, Soviet rule threatened the world with nuclear war.

After World War II (1939–1945), Soviet communism spread. Many countries of Eastern Europe became communist. They were part of the communist empire ruled from Moscow. The Soviet Union grew very powerful. It built a huge army, navy, and air force. The Soviet Union wanted to spread communism all over the world.

The United States also wanted to promote its system around the world. It also built up its military to do so. From 1945 to the late 1980s was a very tense time. This period is known as the Cold War. Nikita Khrushchev was the Soviet leader at the height of the Cold War. He threatened the United States. He said, "We will bury you." This meant that communism would destroy our economic system. His statement was an opinion, not a fact. His threats never came true.

The end of the Soviet Union was closely tied to the fall of communism. Soviet rule ended on Christmas Day 1991. Soldiers pulled down the national flag, featuring a red hammer and sickle. It was on top of the Kremlin, the seat of Soviet power. Then the soldiers put up a new flag. It was the white, blue, and red flag of old Russia.

Today the Soviet Union is buried. It is dead—a part of history.

Adapted from "The Soviet Union: 1922–1991,"
Current Events (volume 91, issue 14)

....

Circle the best answer for each question.

1. Which statement is *not* a fact about conditions during the 1800s?

   (1) Factory owners hired children.

   (2) Factories were dirty and filled with smoke.

   (3) People worked six days a week.

   (4) Workers used their power to end poverty.

2. In Karl Marx's opinion, what was the best economic system?

   (1) a system in which the rich get richer

   (2) a system in which the poor get poorer

   (3) a system in which everyone shares the wealth equally

   (4) a system in which workers overthrow the government

3. During the height of the Cold War, what was Khrushchev's opinion?

   (1) Communism would destroy the U.S. economic system.

   (2) The Soviet Union's armies would take over the world.

   (3) The United States was stronger than the Soviet Union.

   (4) The Soviet Union would bury countries in Eastern Europe.

4. What happened on December 25, 1991?

   (1) Lenin set up the first communist government.

   (2) The Soviet Union went out of existence.

   (3) Kremlin soldiers celebrated Christmas.

   (4) Old Russia became the Soviet Union.

Check your answers on page 159.

Exercise 3

Read the passage and complete the exercise that follows.

Why do people go to lawyers? What should people do if they are injured in an accident?

Should People Sue So Much?

In the United States, it's easy for people to take their problems to court. In no other country can people get such big awards.

Americans clog the courts with one million tort claims a year. A **tort** is a claim made because someone has been injured. Harm may have been done on purpose. Harm may also result from being careless.

Debate rages over whether the U.S. tort system is good or bad. Doctors say that they are hurt by lawsuits. Companies that make products feel the same way. Insurance rates have soared to cover claims.

Michael Maher is president of the Trial Lawyers of America. He sees another side of the issue. This is his opinion: "The big awards send a strong message to those who make unsafe products, cheat customers, and hide hazards." That message is "Act responsibly."

The tort system wasn't always like this. Fewer lawsuits were filed thirty years ago. Fewer were won. Insurance was cheap. But not everyone could afford to hire a lawyer.

Around 1960, the system began to change. For the first time, some courts allowed lawyers to accept contingency fees. These are fees that clients pay only if their lawyer wins a case. That meant that poor people could sue more easily. By 1965, all fifty states allowed lawyers to accept contingency fees.

The growing number of cars also changed how people felt about suing. That is Lawrence Friedman's view. He teaches law at Stanford University. He feels that car accidents brought ordinary people to court. Juries felt sorry for accident victims so they were willing to force insurance companies to pay big awards. Over time, awards became huge.

In the 1970s, insurance companies began to revolt. They canceled some policies. They hiked premiums for others. As a result, some doctors stopped delivering babies. Some towns closed their swimming pools. Doctors and park districts were afraid of malpractice suits. If they were sued, they might have to pay so much money in damages that they would be forced out of business.

Today, critics of the tort system urge change. They want to make it harder for Americans to sue.

Adapted from "Should People Sue So Much?"
News for You, October 9, 1991

. . . .

Circle *F* for a fact or *O* for an opinion.

F   O   **1.** A tort is a claim someone makes because of an injury.

F   O   **2.** The U.S. tort system is good.

F   O   **3.** Big awards send a strong message to those who make unsafe products.

F   O   **4.** People filed fewer lawsuits thirty years ago.

F   O   **5.** Contingency fees mean that clients pay only if their lawyer wins a case.

F   O   **6.** Cars have changed people's feelings about suing.

F   O   **7.** Today, some people want changes in the U.S. tort system.

Check your answers on page 159.

WRITING WORKSHOP

Brainstorm: Make a List
In this chapter, you read a letter to the editor on pages 60–61. What is your opinion of handguns? Do people have a right to own them? Or do you think handguns should be outlawed? Make a list of your views on this topic.

Focus: Write a Topic Sentence
Write a sentence summarizing your view of handguns. Your sentence should clearly state your opinion.

Expand: Write a Letter to the Editor
Write a letter to the editor of your local newspaper. Give reasons to support your opinion. Try to use facts to show why you think your views are correct.

CHAPTER 9 | INFERENCES

Suppose you have just gone on a job interview. The interviewer smiles and shakes your hand. Then she says, "I'm very impressed with your skills. You're the kind of person we like to hire. I'll call you next week. I will tell you my decision then."

What do the interviewer's comments suggest? Can you "read between the lines"? The interviewer did not directly say, "You have a good chance of getting the job." However, she gave you hints that this is what she meant. Using clues to guess what someone is suggesting is called **making an inference**.

■ Try your skill at reading between the lines. During the Vietnam War, many Americans marched in the streets. They carried signs with statements such as these:

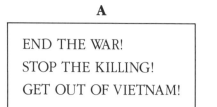

A	B
END THE WAR! STOP THE KILLING! GET OUT OF VIETNAM!	USA ALL THE WAY! BOMB NORTH VIETNAM! AMERICA—LOVE IT OR LEAVE IT!

Which column has the signs carried by those who supported the war? _____
Which column has the signs carried by those who were against the war? _____

The signs in **column B** all suggest that the U.S. government was **doing the right thing** by fighting in the Vietnam War. In contrast, the signs in **column A suggest the opposite**.

As you read the following passage, look for clues about the author's opinion of how Vietnam veterans were treated.

Coming Home

Vietnam Veterans Memorial

Vietnam veterans were not welcomed home with parades in the 1970s. In fact, they were often ignored or booed. America seemed embarrassed that it could not win this war. The government seemed to think that if it ignored the veterans' physical and emotional problems, they would go away on their own. Vietnam veterans became very angry at how they were treated.

Finally, in November 1982 Vietnam veterans

were welcomed home with a victory parade. Architect Maya Lin designed the Vietnam Veterans Memorial in Washington, D.C. It is one of the most-visited monuments in the capital. Its black granite wall bears the name of every soldier who was killed or listed as missing in the Vietnam War. Many visitors come to grieve for loved ones who were lost in the war. And with the pain has come healing.

....

■ The author's opinion about how Vietnam veterans were treated is not directly stated in the passage. On the lines below, write three clues that show how veterans were treated unfairly.

1. _____

2. _____

3. _____

Here are the clues in the passage: **Vietnam veterans were not welcomed home with a parade**; **veterans were often ignored or booed**; **the government ignored their physical and emotional problems**.

STRATEGY: HOW TO MAKE INFERENCES

▶ Look for clues. Find the topic, main idea, and details.
▶ Figure out why the author included certain details.
▶ Read between the lines. What do the details suggest?
▶ Check to see if you have enough information to make the inference.

Exercise 1

Read the passage and complete the exercise that follows.

How do you decide which candidate to vote for in an election? Do you usually vote for a Democrat or a Republican? Why?

What Is a Democrat?

John F. Kennedy

Mark Brown is a union official. He says, "Millions of people used to be proud to say, 'I'm a Democrat.' They used to fight over it. They used to drink over it. They used to laugh over it. They used to argue over it." Brown thinks that times have changed. The number of Democrats seems to have fallen. And he wonders why.

People used to know the answer to this question: "What is a Democrat?" Past presidents were clear examples. Franklin Roosevelt, Harry Truman, and John Kennedy were Democrats. They knew what being a Democrat was all about.

Here are some things that Mark Brown says the Democratic Party believes in:

- the middle class
- factory workers and unions
- the civil rights of minorities and women
- a strong defense
- social welfare programs

In the 1990s, the party must define what being a Democrat means today. Many people are worried about the economy. Today's Democratic Party seems more **moderate**[1] than it did in the past. Party members are stressing investment and growth. They want to build bridges between them and business. They want to pump up the economy. Democrats also want to stop crime by putting more police on the streets. Uniting the party is a chief aim. This is the new face of the Democratic Party.

During the 1980s, voters chose Republican presidents. Mark Brown wants that pattern to change. "We've got our work cut out for us to bring these people home. We have to find the right message and the right messenger."

---

¹moderate: avoiding extremes

Circle the best answer for each question.

1. In the first paragraph, what do Mark Brown's remarks suggest about Democrats in the past?
   (1) Democrats enjoyed going to bars.
   (2) Democrats used to be proud of their party.
   (3) Democrats had bad tempers.
   (4) Democrats liked to tell jokes.

2. What does the passage suggest about Franklin Roosevelt, Harry Truman, and John Kennedy?
   (1) Their ideas and actions confused people.
   (2) They were strong leaders who understood their roles as Democratic presidents.
   (3) They would not know how to solve the problems of the 1990s.
   (4) They ignored the needs of business.

3. What can you infer about Democrats running for president in the 1980s?
   (1) They were not able to gain the trust of the majority of voters.
   (2) They spent too much money on their political campaigns.
   (3) They were not as smart as the Republicans running for president.
   (4) They did not know how worried people were about the economy.

4. What does "finding the right message and the right messenger" mean?
   (1) a person who can make exciting speeches
   (2) a Democratic president who can define the party's goals
   (3) a means of sending letters to voters' homes
   (4) a leader who talks about stopping crime

5. According to the passage, what are some of the goals of today's Democrats?
   You may check (✓) more than one.
   _____ (1) to stress investment and growth
   _____ (2) to cut all social welfare programs
   _____ (3) to stop crime by putting more police on the streets
   _____ (4) to give big business more tax breaks
   _____ (5) to pump up the economy

   Check your answers on page 159.

Exercise 2

Read the passage and complete the exercise that follows.

How would you feel if your boss searched your desk or locker? Should there be laws to protect your privacy at work?

Privacy Ends at Work

Some call it spying. Others say employers have a right to know. Privacy in the workplace is a growing concern.

Many workers are not protected from these acts:

- Drug tests on short notice
- Searches of desks and lockers
- Being fired for smoking
- Personality tests
- Secret checks on work speed
- Tapping work phones

These privacy issues differ from those of the past. Michael Losey heads the Society for Human Resource Management. He made this comment: "Employers used to ask what kind of car workers drove or whether or not they owned their own homes."

The Society has 70,000 members. It asked nearly 1,500 employers and managers this question: Should employers be checking up on their workers? About 57 percent approved of checking workers' keystrokes. About 49 percent would record workers' calls. And 45 percent said searches of workers' desks, lockers, or offices were okay.

Many workers think the U.S. Constitution is on their side. They believe it protects their privacy at work. Usually, that's not the case. The Constitution can only set limits on government snooping.

Sheribel Rothenberg, a lawyer, said, "Bosses have a right to tap your phone and to check your phone log. It's *their* phone and meant for work use only."

Rothenberg says workers are bringing more lawsuits. Bosses complain about the high cost of defending themselves. But that doesn't mean workers are winning in court. Rothenberg made this statement: "For every worker who wins a case, there are 300 who lose."

How can workers start winning cases? They will have to change the laws.

Adapted from "Privacy Ends at Work," *News for You*, October 30, 1991

. . . .

Circle the best answer for each question.

1. What is the main idea of the passage?
   (1) Bosses hire spies to learn about workers.
   (2) Workers are worried about privacy at their jobs.
   (3) Today's privacy issues are the same as those in the past.
   (4) Workers can be fired for smoking.

2. Based on Sheribel Rothenberg's comments, what can you infer about her views on employers' rights?
   (1) She would support a worker's right to privacy.
   (2) She would defend a boss's right to record workers' phone calls.
   (3) She would advise workers to sue their bosses.
   (4) She would help workers change the laws.

3. What does the passage suggest about laws governing people at work?
   (1) The U.S. Constitution protects workers.
   (2) Laws were made to give workers more power.
   (3) Laws favor the side of bosses.
   (4) Workers receive fair trials in court.

4. Which statement sums up employers' views about workers' rights to privacy?
   (1) All agree it is okay to search workers' desks, lockers, or offices.
   (2) Most agree that an employee can be fired for smoking at work.
   (3) Many agree that drug tests can be given on short notice.
   (4) About half agree that it is okay to check workers' keystrokes and to record workers' calls.

Check your answers on page 159.

Exercise 3

Read the passage and complete the exercise that follows.

What problems do children face in countries all over the world? What political organization has helped needy children?

Caring for the World's Children

Each Halloween, children go trick-or-treating for UNICEF. Every Christmas, many people send UNICEF greeting cards. These are just two ways of raising money for UNICEF. The letters stand for United Nations International Children's Emergency Fund. It is a special agency of the United Nations. UNICEF is devoted to children's needs around the world.

UNICEF was created in 1946. Its goal was to help children in Europe and China. The children were suffering from the effects of World War II. By 1953, most war-torn countries had rebuilt their cities and schools. Their children were able to lead more normal lives.

The United Nations General Assembly has been called the "town meeting of the world." In the 1950s, its members knew that many children in poor countries faced problems. Young people lacked food, homes, education, and health care. So every member of the United Nations voted to keep UNICEF active.

Today, UNICEF helps children in over 100 countries. The agency does this in many ways. UNICEF provides milk and vitamins for new mothers and their babies. It trains parents to care for their children's health and safety.

UNICEF workers also look for cheap, healthy foods that can be easily supplied to poor children. In Algeria, for example, UNICEF invented a powder made from dried milk, vitamins, and other things. The powder can be mixed with other foods to make them more nourishing. UNICEF also developed a simple mix of salts. This mix, added to water, feeds sick babies. The mix costs only pennies. It has already saved many lives.

Adapted from *The United Nations*, by Harold and Geraldine Woods

Write the clues that support each inference.

1. Both children and adults can help the cause of UNICEF.

   Clues: _____

   _____

2. Members of the United Nations all shared this belief: They had a political responsibility to help children.

   Clues: _____

   _____

3. UNICEF is concerned with the way children are raised.

   Clues: _____

   _____

4. UNICEF tries to solve the problem of world hunger.

   Clues: _____

   _____

Check your answers on page 159.

WRITING WORKSHOP

Brainstorm: Take Notes

Watch a TV news show of people discussing political issues. During the show, take notes on their comments. Listen very closely to people's statements. (*Tip: Check the TV listings for a news show that seems interesting to you.*)

Focus: Summarize the Main Points

Review your notes on the news show. Then briefly summarize the most important points of the discussion.

Expand: Make Inferences

What did people's comments on the news show suggest about their views? What inferences did they make about a political issue? Write a paragraph answering these questions. Include facts or details that support the inferences.

CHAPTER 10 | PREDICTING OUTCOMES

Before you watch a football game, do you predict who will be the winner? Sports reporters often do. They look at the strengths and weaknesses of each team. They focus on the coaches and key players. They also review each team's win-loss record. Then, based on their knowledge, sports announcers predict the outcome of the game.

Predicting an outcome means guessing what might happen. You can apply this skill when you read social studies passages. Writers often make predictions based on their knowledge of past events. They notice how facts and events are related. Also, authors sometimes give enough information for you to make your own predictions.

In political science, polling is one method of attempting to predict an outcome. Polls are surveys of people's opinions. During an election year, polls report voters' views. The information in the polls are clues about the future. These clues are used to guess what might happen: Which candidates do voters prefer? Who will win the election? Who will lose?

As you read the following passage, look for clues that will help you make a prediction.

Women's Future in Politics

How do voters view women? Many think of women as political outsiders because they are not closely tied to the main group in power. However, in the 1990s women in politics are gaining strength.

U.S. Senator Carol Moseley-Braun

In 1992, surveys were taken of people's opinions. They compared women politicians with men politicians. The results were that people feel that the women
- are more honest, caring, and moral
- respond more to the concerns of voters
- are more likely to involve others in the political process
Women politicians also were rated better than men politicians on social issues. These issues include welfare, health care, and education.

The voters' first concern is the economy. Many seem willing to let women try to fix the mess. Douglas Muzzio, a political scientist at Baruch College in New York City, says, "They can't do much worse than the men."

Many voters seem open to the idea of women in high offices. In a poll by the Times-Mirror Center, 69 percent agreed with this statement: The United States would "be better off if more women served in Congress."

....

■ Answer the questions in the space provided.

What did Douglas Muzzio predict about women's ability to solve the problems of the economy?

_____

You were correct if you wrote this statement: **Women "can't do much worse than the men."**
Now it's your turn to predict an outcome. Based on the passage, make a prediction about women's future in politics.

_____

_____

Perhaps you wrote that: **many more women will become members of Congress**. The results of the polls and surveys show this is a likely outcome. Of course, other predictions are possible.

STRATEGY: HOW TO PREDICT OUTCOMES

▶ Apply what you already know about the topic.
▶ Notice the clues the author gives you. How are the facts or events related? Does the author explain causes and effects?
▶ Use this information to guess what might happen.
▶ Check to see if you have enough information to support your prediction.

Exercise 1

Read the passage and complete the exercise that follows.

Should nuclear weapons be banned? Do you know how many countries have nuclear weapons?

The Threat of Nuclear Weapons

The United States and other world powers are fighting a battle to stop the spread of nuclear weapons. Are they winning or losing the battle?

Everyone is worried about the spread of nuclear weapons. The reasons are very clear. The more nations that have nuclear weapons, the more likely it is that these weapons will be used.

In 1945, only *one* nation had nuclear weapons. By 1949, *two* nations had nuclear weapons. By 1964, *five* nations had them. Today, *eight* nations admit having nuclear weapons:

| United States | Russia* | France | China |
| Great Britain | Ukraine* | Kazakhstan* | Belarus* |

The starred (*) nations have broken off from the former Soviet Union. Four other nations are believed to have a store of nuclear weapons. They are India, Pakistan, South Africa, and Israel. But these countries won't admit it. Experts say that twenty other nations are trying to make nuclear weapons.

Experts in the United States are most concerned with four nations. They are Libya, North Korea, Iran, and Algeria. Why do these countries pose a threat? The Soviet Union broke apart in 1991. The United States fears that the former Soviet nuclear scientists may help these four nations become nuclear powers.

Three of the four nations are in very tense parts of the world. Iran, Algeria, and Libya are enemies of Israel. Israel has already fought four wars with its Arab neighbors. What if the entire Middle East had nuclear weapons? Experts have made this prediction: The next Middle East war could be fought with nuclear weapons.

"It doesn't take much imagination," said Senator Alan Cranston, "to [understand] what would happen if all these nations [got] nuclear weapons."

Adapted from "Nukes on the Loose," *Current Events*, volume 92, issue 19

. . . .

Circle the best answer for each question.

1. Why did the author list all the nations with nuclear weapons?

   (1) to show the spread of nuclear weapons

   (2) to name the nations that were part of the Soviet Union

   (3) to explain the enemies of the United States

   (4) to show how countries have become more modern

2. According to the passage, what is one possible outcome of the Soviet Union's downfall?

   (1) The United States no longer needs to be afraid of the Soviet Union.

   (2) Russian nuclear scientists will lose their jobs.

   (3) Former Soviet scientists may help four nations become nuclear powers.

   (4) Israel will probably benefit from the Soviet Union's collapse.

3. In the fifth paragraph, what prediction did experts make?

   (1) All Arab countries will make more nuclear weapons.

   (2) The next Middle East war could be fought with nuclear weapons.

   (3) Iran, Algeria, and Libya will all declare war on Israel.

   (4) A nuclear war could destroy the world.

4. It is an opinion that *which* country has nuclear weapons?

   (1) France

   (2) China

   (3) South Africa

   (4) Algeria

Check your answers on pages 159–160.

Exercise 2

Read the passage and complete the exercise that follows.

What would you do if you weren't allowed to play high school sports? How have laws affected women's right to compete in sports?

A Victory for Women Athletes

There is a small dairy town called Wishkah Valley, located in the state of Washington. In September 1973, three high school girls from this town were featured in a news story. They were Delores Darrin, her sister Carol, and Kathy Tosland. This headline appeared in the *Star-News*, a newspaper in Washington, D.C.: "Yes, Delores Is a Guard." Under the headline was a picture of Delores. She was wearing a padded football jersey and a helmet. Beside the picture was a comment from Carol: "None of the other guys at school would turn out, so we figured the team needed us."

All three girls were expected to make sports history. They were going to play on their school's varsity football team. Instead, they made legal history. A ruling kept them off the field. They fought the ruling in court.

The Washington Interscholastic Activities Association (WIAA) wouldn't allow women to play in a football game involving men. John Wolfe and other members of the American Civil Liberties Union (ACLU) of Washington had been following the events at Wishkah Valley. The ACLU had been keeping track of new court orders. These orders had granted women the right to compete against men in sports such as golf, skiing, and tennis.

Wolfe took the girls' case to court. He listed recent laws that protected women's rights in education, politics, economics, and sports. Wolfe fought a long legal battle.

In September 1975, the Supreme Court of Washington reached a decision. Five of the nine judges signed a statement that said high school students couldn't be denied the right to play on the school's football team because they were girls. This would be "discrimination based on sex." Therefore, it was not allowed.

Thousands of girls and women across the country were happy about the decision. Other women—and men—were not. Many coaches and school officials predicted that the court's decision could mean the end of all school athletics. Some felt this question was still unsettled: What is women's place in sports?

By 1980, girls made up one-third of all high school athletes. This number had increased six times during the early seventies. Their numbers are still growing.

....

PART A

Circle the best answer for the question.

1. What prediction did the *Star-News* make about Delores, Carol, and Kathy?
   (1) that the girls would not be accepted on the team
   (2) that the girls would be asked to leave the school
   (3) that the girls would play on the varsity football team
   (4) that the girls should take their request to court

PART B

Answer the questions in the space provided.

1. What was the outcome of the case brought before the Supreme Court of Washington?

   _____

   _____

   _____

2. What did some coaches and school officials predict as a result of the state Supreme Court's decision?

   _____

   _____

3. Make a prediction about the future of women athletes. Base your prediction on information in the passage and your own experience.

   _____

   _____

Check your answers on page 160.

Exercise 3

Read the passage and complete the exercise that follows.

Why is TV so important during an election year? How do today's candidates run their campaigns?

Modern Campaigns for President

Running for president has greatly changed in the last fifty years. Every part of campaigning has been touched. The main cause of these changes is the *cost* of getting elected. Candidates must now depend on the mass media. The mass media are TV, radio, newspapers, and magazines. TV can reach millions of people. But the rates for TV time would shock politicians from the past.

1992 Presidential Debate

Changes in laws have affected campaigns. These laws control ways of spending money. In 1974, amendments to the Federal Election Campaign Act allowed public funds to be used for candidates running for president. But the cost of campaigns can lead to misuse of the funds. Candidates often try to avoid the rules. This is because they need to keep raising more money. Much of the money is spent to buy TV time.

With each recent election, TV has grown in importance. Candidates appear on the nightly news. They are guests on interview shows. They appear in campaign ads. They debate on TV. Some two-thirds of all voters rely on TV to tell them about the candidates and issues. "Politics is show business," said Joe Klein in *New York* magazine. " 'Running for President' is a show that airs once a day . . . just before 'Wheel of Fortune' or the evening news."

TV is designed mainly to sell products. It has always searched for a message people will like. Doubts and questions will not sell toothpaste or soap. Messages must be simple and repeated often. No wonder political campaigns annoy and bore people. This stops the better candidates from running.

Adapted from *Campaigns and Elections*, by George Sullivan

Circle the best answer for each question.

1. According to the passage, what is the main cause for the change in campaigns for president?
   (1) the way products are sold on TV
   (2) the cost of getting elected
   (3) the new laws that were passed
   (4) the wrong use of funds

2. Which of the following statements best explains why TV affects the outcome of an election?
   (1) Some voters watch candidates on interview shows.
   (2) Most voters depend on TV for news about candidates.
   (3) Politics is show business.
   (4) Campaign ads bore TV viewers.

3. Based on the passage, what is an outcome resulting from the way political campaigns are run today?
   (1) Better candidates will choose not to run.
   (2) More people will vote in elections.
   (3) Rates for TV time will keep increasing.
   (4) Candidates will spend less money during their campaigns.

Check your answers on page 160.

WRITING WORKSHOP

Brainstorm: Ask Questions
In this chapter, you read the results of polls about women in politics. Find out what your friends think about women politicians. Write a list of questions you will ask them. Reread the passage on pages 76–77 to help you get some ideas.

Focus: State the Purpose of the Poll
Write a statement describing exactly what you hope to learn from the poll. For example, is your goal to find out if more people plan to vote for women? Do you want to compare and contrast the political skills of men and women?

Expand: Predict Outcomes
Ask your friends to answer the questions on your poll. Summarize their responses. Then, based on the results of your survey, make predictions about the future of women in politics.

CHAPTER 11 | POLITICAL CARTOONS

The purpose of comic strips is to make you laugh or to tell a story. You look at the characters and read what they say.

The purpose of many **political cartoons** is also to make you laugh. However, political cartoons have a serious purpose, too. Through pictures and words, they comment about current events. Like letters to the editor, political cartoons give an opinion.

■ Study the political cartoon. First, read the background notes. They tell you information about the subject of the cartoon. Then read the labels on the car and trucks and the words the characters are saying. The notes below explain details about the cartoon.

Background: In the early 1990s, many people in the United States were unhappy about how the government was handling the economy. It was a key issue in the 1992 elections.

- The **elephant** is a symbol of the **Republican Party**.
- "**G.O.P.**" stands for **Grand Old Party** (another name for the **Republican Party**).
- The **donkey** is a symbol of the **Democratic Party**.
- "**DEM.**" means **Democrats**.
- The **man** is **Uncle Sam**. He is a symbol of the United States. He usually has white hair and a beard and wears a top hat.

Remember that the characters are symbols. A **symbol** stands for something. Uncle Sam, the elephant, and the donkey appear in many political cartoons.

■ Describe what is happening in the cartoon.

1. What kind of trucks are the Democratic Party and Republican Party driving?

_____

2. What is wrong with the car labeled U.S. economy?

_____

3. What are both political parties trying to do?

_____

4. What can you infer from the characters' spoken words?

_____

_____

5. Why do you think the cartoonist has both the DEM and the G.O.P. saying the same words at the same time?

_____

The answers are: **1. They are driving tow trucks**; **2. the car (the economy) is falling apart**; **3. to tow the car in different directions**; **4. both parties think they can fix the economy**; **5. both parties often claim they have the _right_ solution, even though their solutions differ**.

Understanding political cartoons is like putting together the pieces of a puzzle. All the parts make up the total picture, or the meaning.

STRATEGY: HOW TO UNDERSTAND POLITICAL CARTOONS

▶ Notice every detail of the cartoon.
▶ Look at the characters. Who are they? What are they saying?
▶ Read every word in the cartoon. Study the labels and descriptions.
▶ Figure out if any pictures are symbols. What do you think they mean?
▶ Check to see if your inferences about the cartoon make sense.

Exercise 1

Read the background notes and the cartoon.

Why are medical bills so high? Do you think the government needs to change the health-care system?

The Politics of Health Care

Background: Health-care costs keep increasing. Many people cannot afford to see a doctor. This is because medical insurance costs too much money. The government also has cut back the money to help poor people pay for medical costs.

Some politicians want the government to control the soaring costs. They also believe all Americans deserve good health care. Health care was a major issue during the 1992 elections.

Answer the questions in the space provided.

1. According to the background notes, why do some politicians believe the government should control health-care costs?

   _____

2. According to the background notes, why can't some people afford to see a doctor?

   _____

3. What is the label on the side of the wheelchair?

   _____

4. What are the other labels in the cartoon?

   _____

5. What have the two men done to the wheelchair?

   _____

6. How will having no wheels affect the man in the wheelchair?

   _____

7. What might happen to poor people who lose government aid for health care? Base your prediction on the details in the cartoon.

   _____

   _____

   _____

Check your answers on page 160.

Exercise 2

Read the background notes and the cartoon.

In the 1920s, President Calvin Coolidge made this famous comment: "The business of America is business." Are Americans too interested in finding ways to earn profits? Are there businesses that you think are making money for the wrong reason?

The Business Side of War

Background: "War is hell" is a saying that describes soldiers' experiences. In this unit, you read about what happened to Vietnam veterans. They did not receive a hero's welcome after they returned home. Many Americans thought the Vietnam War was a waste. They did not support the soldiers who fought in the war.

In January 1991, the United States fought a war in the Persian Gulf. The war was also called "Operation Desert Storm." Americans welcomed the soldiers from this war when they came back home. Parades across the nation honored their return. Stores carried all kinds of Desert Storm products.

Answer the questions in the space provided.

1. What are some of the products sold in this store? How much do they cost?

   _____

   _____

2. What symbol does the cartoonist use for the man's eyes? Why?

   _____

3. What is the man in the picture doing?

   _____

   _____

4. What words in the cartoon describe what he is thinking?

   _____

   _____

5. Why does the the word *SELL* begin with *$*?

   _____

   _____

   _____

6. What comment does the cartoon make about the man's business?

   _____

   _____

Check your answers on page 160.

Exercise 3

Read the background notes and the cartoon.

Do you want a job in the business world? What might stop your chances for success?

Equal Opportunity?

Background: For over 20 years, women and minorities have struggled for equal pay. They have also fought for a fair chance to succeed in jobs. But both groups still earn less than white men in almost every type of job.

"Corporate America" is another name for the business world. In this world, men are in power. Very few women and minorities hold top positions in the biggest American companies. Women and minorities say there is a "**glass ceiling**." This phrase means that they are kept from advancing to the highest positions.

Answer the questions in the space provided.

1. What does the man in the cartoon stand for?

_____

2. What does the man look like? Write a brief description.

_____

_____

_____

3. Two doors are opened in the cartoon. What labels are above each doorway?

_____

4. What is behind the door on the left?

_____

5. What is behind the door on the right?

_____

6. Based on the cartoon, is the man telling the truth? Why or why not?

_____

_____

Check your answers on page 160.

WRITING WORKSHOP

Brainstorm: Make a List

Find a political cartoon in the newspaper. Study it closely. Then write a list of phrases describing the cartoon. Your list should include many details.

Focus: Create a Title

Think about what the cartoon is saying. Then write a title. The title should state the topic of the cartoon.

Expand: Write a Paragraph

Organize your list of phrases into a paragraph. Your paragraph should create a "word picture" of the cartoon. Try to explain the meaning of your description.

UNIT 3
REVIEW

Read the passage and complete the exercises that follow.

Who are terrorists? Why do people all over the world fear them?

The Threat of Terrorism

President John Kennedy once made this comment: "Terror is not a new weapon. Throughout history, it was used by those who could not [win] either by persuasion or example." He was saying that terrorism is a tool of people without power.

Terrorists use violence. They take people hostage. They hijack airplanes. They bomb and shoot. These are some of their methods for gaining power. Through violence, they try to force governments or groups to change. Many of the victims are innocent bystanders. Most terrorists have political and social causes. Terrorists often want to make their causes known. They use the media to gain attention.

Many people share this opinion: TV should not report on terrorist activities. They should not be allowed to spread their political beliefs. Also, "copycat" terrorists may want the same publicity for their cause. Others disagree with this view. They say that the United States is a democracy. Thus, TV has a right to report the news, and Americans have a right to know about events.

What if terrorists were kept off TV? Some people predict that this might cause greater problems. Terrorists might commit worse crimes. It is possible that even more people could get killed.

PART A
Circle the best answer for each question.

1. What can you infer from President Kennedy's remark?
  (1) Terrorists set an example for others to follow.
  (2) People without power use terrorism as a weapon.
  (3) Terrorists know how to persuade others.
  (4) Terrorists have developed new weapons.

2. Which of the following statements is *not* a fact?

   (1) Terrorists use people as hostages.

   (2) Many terrorists have political causes.

   (3) Terrorists try to spread their beliefs.

   (4) Force is the only way to change a government.

3. According to the passage, what do some people think might happen if terrorists were not allowed on TV?

   (1) Terrorists might commit even more serious crimes.

   (2) The United States might no longer be a democracy.

   (3) The use of terrorism might stop.

   (4) Everyone might ignore the problem of terrorism.

PART B

Look at the drawing and circle the best answer for each question.

1. What do you think the terrorist in the drawing is doing?

   (1) shooting a gun at the camera operator

   (2) making a commercial about guns

   (3) making sure that the TV camera focuses on him as he speaks

   (4) talking about the need for gun control

2. Which idea from the passage best describes the opinion expressed in the political drawing?

   (1) Terrorists carry guns to shoot people.

   (2) Terrorists use TV to gain attention.

   (3) Americans want to know about terrorism.

   (4) More people will die if terrorists are kept off TV.

Check your answers on page 160.

UNIT 4
GEOGRAPHY

Geography is the study of places around the world. It looks at people's relationships with the part of the world in which they live.

Geographers work with a variety of maps. Maps help you better understand geography. A map is a drawing of a place that shows you where things are located. By reading maps, you can explore areas of the world you have never visited. Maps also show you special information about geography. They show physical features, population patterns, borders between countries or states, and weather patterns.

In this unit, you will learn how to read symbols on maps. You also will learn how to read map keys at the bottom of maps. These keys help you interpret the information presented in maps.

GEOGRAPHY
TOPICS

- Percentage of Adults Who Can and Cannot Read
- How to Read a Weather Map
- Where Indian Reservations Are Located
- Routes to O'Hare International Airport
- Main Routes of Migrant Workers
- The Freedom Ride
- Where Early Immigrants Settled
- Women's Voting Rights in 1914
- California Missions from 1769 to 1848
- Finding Railroad Lines on a Map

AFTER READING THIS UNIT, YOU SHOULD BE ABLE TO
▶ USE A MAP KEY
▶ FIND DISTANCES AND DIRECTIONS ON A MAP
▶ UNDERSTAND HISTORICAL MAPS

CHAPTER 12 | MAP KEYS

A **symbol** is a picture or a design that stands for something. Every day you see symbols that give you information.

NO SMOKING

HANDICAPPED PARKING ONLY

SCHOOL CROSSING

Map symbols are a kind of language that includes pictures, colors, patterns, or shapes that have a special meaning on a map.

A **map key**, or **legend**, explains the meaning of the symbols. Look for the key in the corner of the map.

Study the map of the world. One symbol in the key stands for the percentage (%) of adults who cannot read. The other symbol shows the percentage (%) of adults who can read.

Percentage of Adults Who Can and Cannot Read

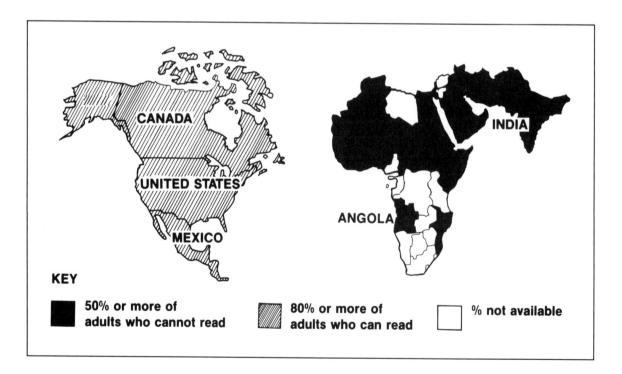

KEY

| ■ | 50% or more of adults who cannot read | ▨ | 80% or more of adults who can read | □ | % not available |

■ Fill out this chart with information from the map.

Country	% of Adults Can Read	% of Adults Cannot Read
United States	80% or more	20% or less
India		
Angola		
Canada		
Mexico		

The correct answers are: **In India and Angola, about 50% (or one-half) of the adults can read, while about 50% (or one-half) of the adults cannot read. In Canada and Mexico, about 80% of the adults can read, while about 20% of the adults cannot read.**

> ## STRATEGY: USING A MAP KEY
>
> ▶ Study the symbols in the map key. What does each symbol represent?
> ▶ Find the location of the symbols on the map.
> ▶ Check how the map symbols are used to explain information.

Exercise 1

Use the map and the notes to complete the exercise that follows.

How does the weather affect your daily life? What useful information can you find on weather maps?

Weather Map

Background notes: Many newspapers print a weather map every day. The key on the weather map helps you understand weather patterns across the country.

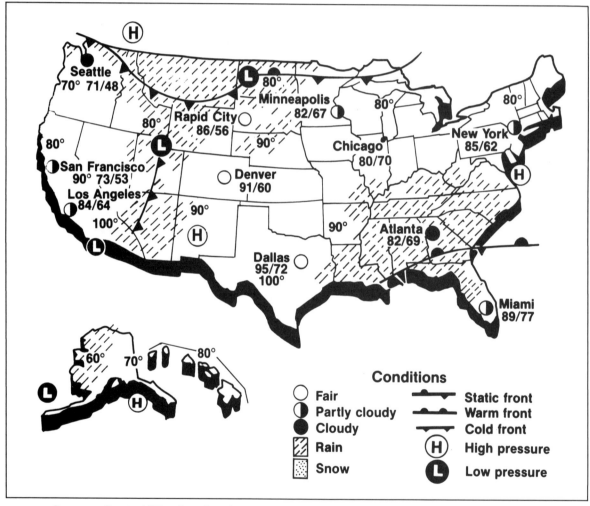

Source: Central Weather Service

Answer the questions in the space provided.

1. What cities on the map have fair skies?

_____   _____

_____

2. What cities on the map have partly cloudy skies?

_____   _____

_____   _____

_____

3. What cities on the map have cloudy skies?

_____   _____

4. What cities on the map are located closest to a cold front?

_____   _____

5. The high temperature in Miami is 89°. What is the low temperature?

_____

6. The low temperature in San Francisco is 53°. What is the high temperature?

_____

7. Which city has a higher temperature—Seattle or Denver?

_____

8. What state do you live in? According to the map, is it raining in your state?

_____

Check your answers on page 161.

Exercise 2

Use the map and the notes to complete the exercise that follows.

Why do people from the same background choose to live together?
Where do Native Americans live?

Indian Lands

Background notes: An Indian reservation is public land set aside for Native Americans. One-third of all Native Americans live on reservations. Some reservations in the United States are supported by the federal government. Others are supported by state governments. Many Native Americans choose not to live on reservations. They may have weaker ties to their culture than those who live on reservations.

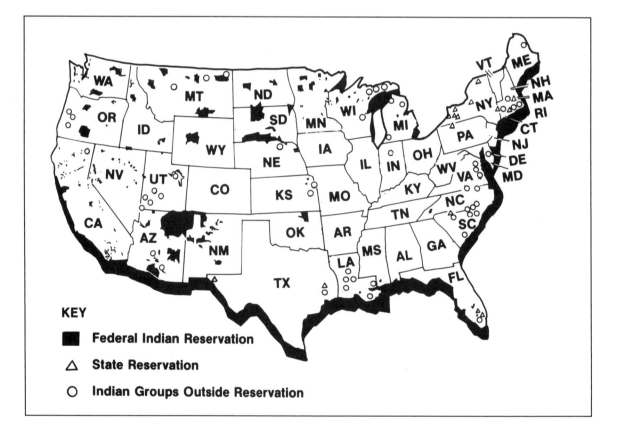

KEY

■ Federal Indian Reservation

△ State Reservation

○ Indian Groups Outside Reservation

Circle the best answer for each question.

1. Where are the most federal Indian reservations located?
   (1) Arizona
   (2) New Mexico
   (3) South Dakota
   (4) North Dakota

2. Which of the following states has the fewest number of Indian groups living outside of reservations?
   (1) Oregon
   (2) Louisiana
   (3) North Carolina
   (4) Utah

3. Where are the greatest number of state reservations located?
   (1) Florida
   (2) South Carolina
   (3) New York
   (4) Maine

Check your answers on page 161.

WRITING WORKSHOP

Brainstorm: Take Notes

In this chapter, you studied the symbols on a weather map. Write notes describing the weather in different parts of the United States. Include temperatures and rainfall in different parts of the country.

Focus: Organize Your Notes

Group your notes according to the symbols on the maps. Also, look for comparisons and contrasts. For example, which city is the hottest? Which city is the coolest?

Expand: Write a Weather Report

Pretend you are a weather reporter on a news show. Write a paragraph summarizing the weather conditions shown on the map. Tell people across the country what kind of weather they can expect. Base your weather report on your notes and the map.

CHAPTER 13 | FINDING DIRECTIONS AND DISTANCES

Have you ever gotten lost by driving in the wrong direction? Have you ever been confused about the distance you had to drive before you reached a certain place? Reading maps can help you figure out both directions and distances.

Routes to O'Hare International Airport

Study the map carefully. The numbers on the map refer to highways.

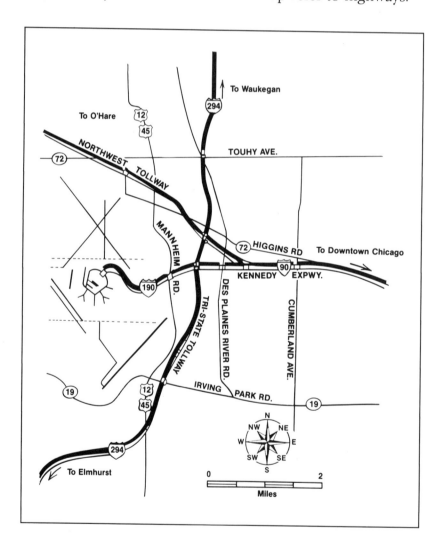

The **directions** are north, south, east, and west. Directions may be marked on maps in a circle or with pointed arrows. Note the compass at the bottom of the map. Each letter stands for a direction: N = north, S = south, E = east, W = west, NE = northeast, NW = northwest, SE = southeast, and SW = southwest.

Real miles are represented on maps by much smaller lengths. A **scale** on a map is a drawing that looks like a small ruler. (Note that a mileage scale is also shown at the bottom of the map.) A scale helps you measure distances on a map: Mark off the distance between two places on the edge of a piece of paper. Then line up the marks on the edge of the paper next to the scale of miles to estimate the distance. This will help you find the distance between two places.

■ Suppose you wanted to drive to O'Hare International Airport. What direction would you travel in if you were leaving from each of these places?

Downtown Chicago _____

Elmhurst _____

Waukegan _____

Here are the correct answers: **northwest**; **north**; and **southwest**.

■ Next, try using the scale on the map to figure out distances. Find Cumberland Avenue. It runs north and south and is located east of the airport. Suppose you are driving on Touhy Avenue and turn on Cumberland Avenue. About how many miles would you travel to reach Irving Park Road? _____

You used the map scale correctly if you wrote **about four miles**. Practice your skill using the scale by measuring other distances on the map.

STRATEGY: HOW TO FIND DIRECTIONS AND DISTANCES

▶ Find the direction symbol on the map. Places at the top of the map are north. Places at the bottom are south. East is to the right, and west is to the left

▶ Find the number of miles represented in the map key.

▶ Practice finding the number of miles on a map from one place to another.

▶ Check to make sure that you have added the number of miles correctly.

Exercise 1

Use the map and the notes to complete the exercise that follows.

What would your life be like if you had to keep moving to support your family? Where do some people go to find work in the United States?

Main Routes of Migrant Workers

Background notes: Migrant workers are people who migrate, or move, often. To find jobs, many families in the United States move several times every year. These families work in the fields. They harvest, or pick, crops by hand. Many migrant workers come from farms in Mexico. They find work in almost every state. The map below shows the routes migrant workers take.

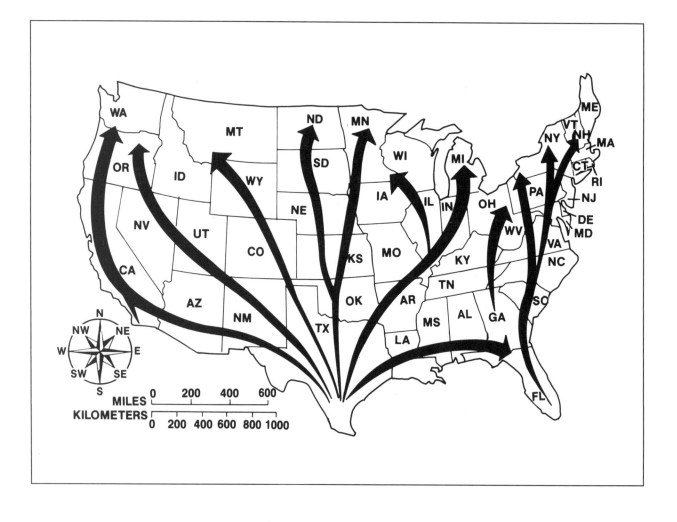

Answer each question in the space provided.

1. In which state do most of the main routes start?

_____

2. In what general direction do most migrant workers travel?

_____

3. About how many miles is the route beginning in Florida and ending in New York?

_____

4. About how many miles is the route beginning in Georgia and ending in Ohio?

_____

5. Which northeastern states are not touched by a migrant route?

_____   _____   _____

6. About how many miles is the route beginning in Texas and ending in Oregon?

_____

7. Which state is the beginning point for the route that ends in Montana?

_____

8. Which four states are beginning points for where two migrant routes branch off?

_____   _____   _____   _____

Check your answers on page 161.

Exercise 2

Use the map and the notes to complete the exercise that follows.

Why did some people take a bus trip in the South called "The Freedom Ride"? What was the purpose of their journey?

The Freedom Ride

Background notes: CORE stands for the Congress of Racial Equality. In 1961, CORE organized the "Freedom Ride." The Freedom Ride was a bus trip. The riders on the trip were African Americans and whites. This was CORE's plan: The African Americans would sit in the front of the bus. If ordered, they would refuse to move to the back of the bus.

The goal of the Freedom Ride was to pressure the government. The Supreme Court had already decided that segregation on buses was illegal. But the government wasn't enforcing this law. People on the bus trip risked their lives for the cause of civil rights.

The first part of the Freedom Ride began in Washington, D.C. The map shows the second part of the Freedom Ride.

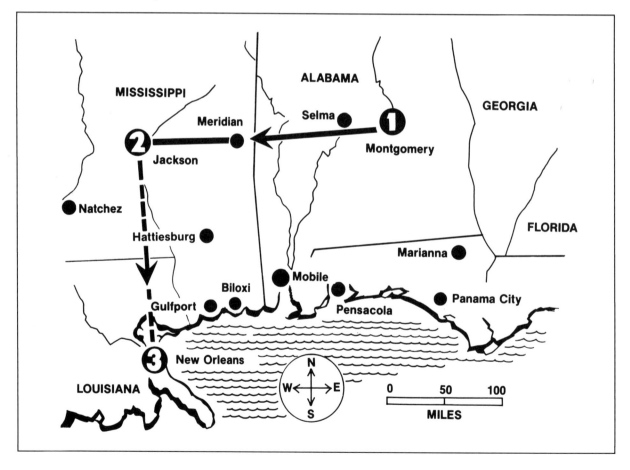

Answer each question in the space provided.

1. The Freedom Ride first headed west and then turned _____.

2. The Freedom Ride traveled through the states of _____, _____, and _____.

3. The distance traveled from Montgomery to Jackson is about _____ miles.

4. The distance traveled from Jackson to New Orleans is about _____ miles.

5. The total distance covered on the second leg of the Freedom Ride was about _____ miles.

6. The distance on the map from Selma to Panama City is about _____ miles.

7. The distance on the map from Biloxi to Montgomery is about _____ miles.

Check your answers on page 161.

WRITING WORKSHOP

Brainstorm: Make a List

Imagine that you are either a migrant worker or a Freedom Rider. Make a list of details describing your journey. Why did you go? What places did you see? What problems did you face? Make up details based on the map on page 104 or the map on page 106.

Focus: Write a Title

Review your list. Then write a title that summarizes your details.

Expand: Write a Travel Diary

Organize your details into a diary, or journal. Make up dates and describe what happened on each of those dates.

CHAPTER 14 | HISTORICAL MAPS

Historical maps help you learn about the past. They can show you what an area looked like many years ago. Some historical maps explain events, trends, or political ideas.

For example, the map that follows helps you better understand the history of immigrants in the United States. Immigrants are people who move from one country to another. Between 1820 and 1920, almost 30 million immigrants came to the United States. Study the map carefully. Find where different immigrant groups first settled.

Where Early Immigrants First Settled

■ Practice your skills in reading the historical map on page 108. Answer the following questions.

1. Which immigrant group first settled in both the East and the West?
   _____

2. In what three states did Mexicans first settle? _____
   _____ _____

3. What immigrant group first settled in Ohio? _____

4. What two immigrant groups first settled near the northern border of the United States? _____ _____

5. In what state did French Canadians first settle? _____

6. Which immigrant group first settled in Massachusetts (MA)?
   _____

7. In what two states did Chinese and Japanese immigrants first settle?
   _____ _____

8. In what four states did Germans first settle?
   _____ _____ _____ _____

9. On what coast did Polish and Russian Jews first settle? _____

Here are the correct answers: **1. Italians**; **2. Arizona, New Mexico, and Texas**; **3. Poles**; **4. Swedes and Norwegians**; **5. Maine**; **6. Irish**; **7. California and Oregon**; **8. Minnesota, Wisconsin, Iowa, and Illinois**; **9. east**.

> ## STRATEGY: HOW TO UNDERSTAND HISTORICAL MAPS
>
> ▶ Read the title and background information. What is the purpose of the map?
> ▶ Read all the words on the map. If the map has a key, locate the symbols on the map.
> ▶ Check to see how the map shows events, trends, or ideas in history.

Exercise 1

Use the map and the notes to complete the exercise that follows.

What would you do if you were denied the right to vote? What steps did women take to gain this right?

Women's Voting Rights: 1914

Background notes: Suffrage means the right to vote. In 1869, the National Women's Suffrage Association was formed. Elizabeth Cady Stanton and Susan B. Anthony headed this group. Their goal was to add an amendment to the Constitution that would give women the right to vote. On March 3, 1913, thousands of women staged a protest. They marched in Washington, D.C., to support suffrage. The suffrage map below is from 1914.

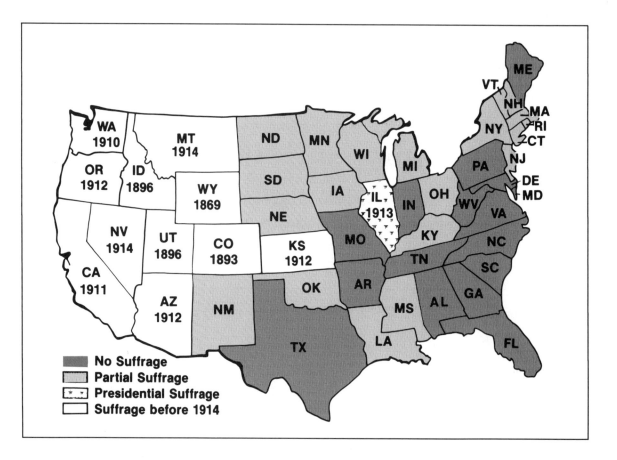

Answer each question in the space provided.

1. What is the subject, or topic, of this map?

_____

2. What was the goal of the National Women's Suffrage Association?

_____

_____

3. (a) In 1911, what 11 states had given women the right to vote?

_____   _____   _____

_____   _____   _____

_____   _____   _____

_____   _____

(b) Where are most of these states located—east, west, north, or south?

_____

4. In which state could a woman vote only for president?

_____

5. List 10 states that denied women the right to vote.

_____   _____

_____   _____

_____   _____

_____   _____

_____   _____

Check your answers on page 161.

Exercise 2

Use the map and the notes to complete the exercise that follows.

Did you know that the names of California's major cities came from the names of missions that were established along the West Coast?

California Missions: 1769–1848

Background notes: In 1769, California was under Spanish rule. Spain established many missions along the West Coast. These missions were settlements run by the Catholic Church. It took about a day to walk from one mission to the next. In 1822, California was brought under Mexican rule.

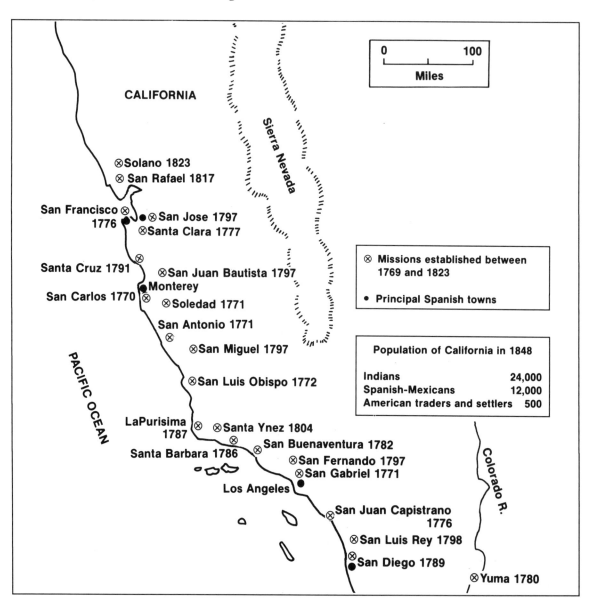

Answer each question in the space provided.

1. How many missions were established before 1800?

_____

2. How many missions were founded after 1800?

_____

3. What town is located directly north of San Carlos?

_____

4. List two missions that became big California cities.

_____   _____

5. What is the approximate distance between San Diego and Santa Barbara?

_____

6. What is the approximate distance between San Francisco and Monterey?

_____

Check your answers on page 161.

WRITING WORKSHOP

Brainstorm: Answer Questions

In this chapter, you studied a map showing where immigrants settled. What country did your ancestors come from? When did they arrive in the United States? Where did they first settle? Where do your relatives live now? Write the answers to these questions.

Focus: Write a Topic Sentence

Write a topic sentence explaining your family's history in the United States.

Expand: Write a Summary

Organize your answers into a paragraph. All the details in your paragraph should relate to the topic sentence, or the main idea. Your paragraph should be a brief history of your family's roots.

UNIT 4
REVIEW

Study the map and notes and complete the exercise that follows.

Who depends on trains today? What was the relationship between railroad lines and cattle trails in the late 1800s?

Moving People and Cattle

Background notes: Cattle ranchers, cowboys, farmers, and railroad workers helped settle the West. Railroads made life easier for cattle ranchers. Cowboys drove herds of cattle to railroad towns. The railroads then shipped the cattle to stockyards in the cities.

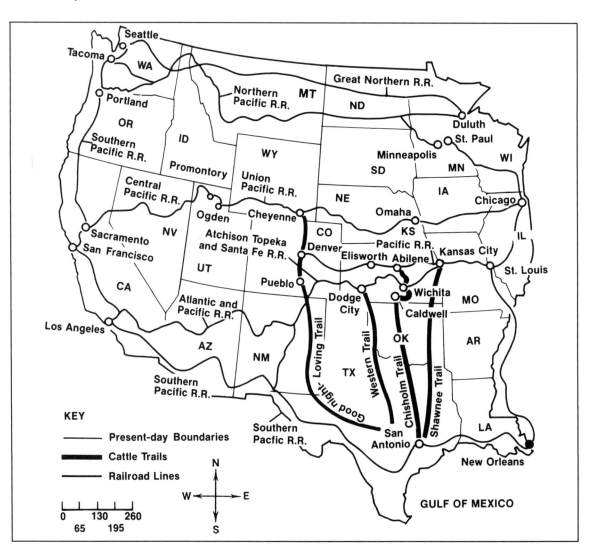

Circle the best answer for each question.

1. What is the name of the longest cattle trail?
   (1) Shawnee Trail
   (2) Chisholm Trail
   (3) Western Trail
   (4) Goodnight-Loving Trail

2. Which railroad traveled north up the California coast?
   (1) Southern Pacific
   (2) Central Pacific
   (3) Atlantic and Pacific
   (4) Northern Pacific

3. How many miles is the Chisholm Trail from San Antonio to Caldwell?
   (1) about 350 miles
   (2) about 400 miles
   (3) about 450 miles
   (4) about 500 miles

4. Which of the following cities was connected to three railroad lines?
   (1) New Orleans
   (2) Chicago
   (3) Dodge City
   (4) Abilene

5. Which of the following was connected to four cattle trails?
   (1) Louisiana
   (2) Kansas City
   (3) San Antonio
   (4) Pueblo

6. Which cattle trail ended in Kansas City?
   (1) Goodnight-Loving Trail
   (2) Western Trail
   (3) Chisholm Trail
   (4) Shawnee Trail

Check your answers on page 161.

UNIT 5
ECONOMICS

What products and services do people buy? How do people earn and spend their money? How do businesses and governments manage money? **Economics** is the branch of the social sciences that addresses these questions.

Information about economics is often presented in charts and graphs. By reading charts and graphs, you can learn important facts and figures.

ECONOMICS
TOPICS

- Jobs That People Keep and Jobs That People Leave
  - What's Important to Workers
  - The Top Salaries and Contracts in Baseball
  - People Without Jobs in the United States
    - Women in the Work Force
  - Education Versus Military Spending
    - Types of Music People Buy
    - Changes in the Work Force
    - Mothers Without Money
    - Where Your Money Goes
    - Who Gets Child Support
  - Amount of Money United States Farmers Earn
    - World Production of Cars
      - Selling *Streetwise*

AFTER READING THIS UNIT, YOU SHOULD BE ABLE TO UNDERSTAND
  ▶ CHARTS
  ▶ LINE GRAPHS
  ▶ BAR GRAPHS
  ▶ CIRCLE GRAPHS

CHAPTER 15 | CHARTS

Charts summarize useful information. Train schedules are charts that tell you about times, fares, and places. The sports sections of the newspapers are filled with charts about teams and players.

Charts are often used in economics to make a set of facts clearer to the reader. The title of a chart usually tells you what the chart is about. The numbers and words in a chart are organized into columns and rows.

For example, the chart below shows how long certain careers last. Notice how the information is arranged.

Jobs That People Keep		Jobs That People Leave	
Job	**Number of Years**	**Job**	**Number of Years**
Barber	24.8	Food-Counter Worker	1.5
Farmer	21.1	Waiter	1.7
Railroad Conductor	18.4	Cashier	2.4
Religious Leader	15.8	Athlete	4.4
Dentist	15.7	Computer Programmer	4.8
Phone Operator	15.0	Author	5.6

Source: U.S. Department of Labor, 1987

■ Practice your skills in reading the chart by answering the following questions.

1. What does the chart compare and contrast?

_____

2. Which career lasts the longest?

_____

3. Which two jobs last less than two years?

_____   _____

4. How long is an athlete's career?

_____

5. Which job lasts longer—waiter or cashier?

_____

6. Which two jobs last more than 20 years?

_____   _____

7. How long is a phone operator's career?

_____

8. Which job do people leave sooner—dentist or railroad conductor?

_____

9. Which job do people keep longer—computer programmer or author?

_____

Here are the answers: **1. The chart compares and contrasts jobs that people keep with jobs that people leave**; **2. barber**; **3. food-counter worker, waiter**; **4. 4.4 years**; **5. cashier**; **6. barber, farmer**; **7. 15 years**; **8. dentist**; **9. author**.

Did you notice that the information on the chart is easy to find? Charts also help you compare and contrast numbers and facts.

STRATEGY: HOW TO READ A CHART

▸ Find the title. What is the topic of the chart?
▸ Read all the headings for the columns and rows. What kinds of information are presented on the chart?
▸ Study all the facts and figures.
▸ Check to see how the facts and figures are related. Look for comparisons and contrasts.

Exercise 1

Study the chart and complete the exercise that follows.

What things do you value the most at your job? Why?

What's Important to Workers		
Job Characteristics	**Very Important (percent of workers)**	**Completely Satisfied (percent of workers)**
Good health insurance and other benefits	81%	27%
Interesting work	78	41
Job security	78	35
The chance to learn new skills	68	31
Yearly vacation of one week or more	66	35
Being able to work without close supervision	64	42
Recognition by co-workers	62	24
Having a job in which you can help others	58	34
Limited job stress	58	18
Regular hours, no nights or weekends	58	40
High salary	56	13
Working close to home	55	46
Work that is important to society	53	34
Chances for promotion	53	20
Contact with a lot of people	52	45

Source: Gallup Poll, 1991

Read each statement. Circle *T* if it is true or *F* if it is false.

T F **1.** The chart shows that most workers are totally satisfied with things they want from their jobs.

T F **2.** Workers feel that good insurance is more important than a high salary.

T F **3.** Workers say that a one-week vacation every year is less important than regular hours.

T F **4.** All the figures under the column heading "Completely Satisfied" are below 50%.

T F **5.** The smallest gap between the two columns of percentages (%) is for "Contact with a lot of people."

T F **6.** Workers say interesting work and job security are equally important.

T F **7.** Only 18% of workers feel that limited job stress is important.

T F **8.** The same percentage (%) of workers say they are completely satisfied with job security and yearly vacation time.

T F **9.** Based on the chart, you can infer that workers think training on the job is not important.

T F **10.** Based on the chart, you can infer that most employers are meeting their workers' needs.

T F **11.** Workers say that recognition by co-workers is more important than learning new skills.

T F **12.** Based on the chart, 34% of workers are completely satisfied that they have a job in which they can help others.

Check your answers on page 162.

Exercise 2

Study the two charts and complete the exercise that follows.

In March 1992, Ryne Sandberg became the highest-paid player in baseball history. What other baseball players earn well over a million dollars a year? Do you think they are worth that much money?

The Top Salaries in Baseball				
Rank	Player	Team	Years	Average Salary
1	Ryne Sandberg	Cubs	1992–96	$7,100,000
2	Bobby Bonilla	Mets	1992–96	$5,800,000
3	Jack Morris	Jays	1992–93	$5,425,000
4	Roger Clemens	Red Sox	1992–95	$5,380,250
5	Dwight Gooden	Mets	1992–94	$5,150,000

Source: The *Chicago Tribune*, March 3, 1992

Important Contracts in Baseball History				
Salary	Player	Team	Year	Contract Length
$1,000,000	Nolan Ryan	Astros	1979	4 years
$2,040,000	George Foster	Mets	1982	5 years
$3,000,000	Kirby Puckett	Twins	1989	3 years
$4,700,000	Jose Canseco	Athletics*	1990	5 years
$5,380,250	Roger Clemens	Red Sox	1991	4 years
$7,100,000	Ryne Sandberg	Cubs	1992	4 years

*The Athletics traded Canseco to the Rangers in 1992.
Source: The *Chicago Tribune*, March 3, 1992

Answer the questions in the space provided.

1. What is Ryne Sandberg's salary for 1993? _____

2. Among those listed in the second chart, who was the first baseball player to sign a contract for $1,000,000 a year? _____

3. Which two baseball players are listed on both charts? _____ _____

4. Which two of the highest-paid baseball players in the 1990s are on the same team? _____   _____

5. Which player signed a three-year contract in 1989? _____

6. How much money did Jack Morris earn in 1992? _____

7. What team offered Jose Canseco a five-year contract in 1990? _____

8. How much money did Kirby Puckett earn in 1989? _____

9. Which two players were offered the longest contracts?

_____   _____

10. Which player signed a four-year contract in 1991 that offered him more than $5,000,000 a year? _____

Check your answers on page 162.

Writing Workshop

Brainstorms: Write a List

Many other professional athletes also make several million dollars a year. Some people think that professional athletes make too much money. Write a list of reasons why you agree or disagree with this statement.

Focus: State Your Point of View

Are you for or against high salaries for professional athletes? State your opinion in a sentence.

Expand: Write a Letter to the Editor

Pretend you are writing a letter to the editor. State your opinion about professional athletes' salaries. Support your opinion with reasons. Try to include facts about salaries from the baseball charts in this chapter.

CHAPTER 16 | LINE GRAPHS

Reading line graphs helps you better understand the facts and figures used in economics. A **line graph** uses a line to show a change, or trend, over a period of time. The line is connected to different points on the graph.

Study the following line graph. Notice how the parts of a line graph are arranged.

Background notes: The title tells you the topic and the time period. The label tells you that the numbers on the bottom of the graph are years. Each notch on the bottom line of the graph represents one year. The label tells you that the numbers on the side of the graph represent the percent (%) of people unemployed. A line slanted upward shows an increase. A line slanted downward shows a decrease.

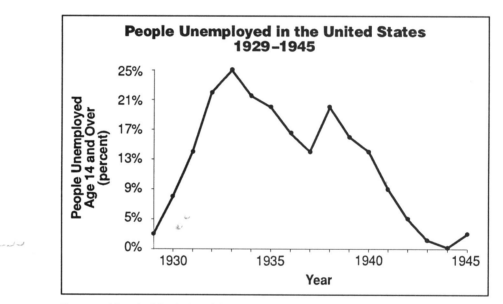

Source: *Historical Statistics of the United States, Colonial Times to 1970*

Remember to read the title and labels first before you try to find specific facts.

■ How would you find the highest percent of people without jobs in 1933? Put your finger on the year 1933 on the bottom of the graph. Then move your finger straight up until you reach the highest peak of the line. Next, read across to the number on the left side of the graph.
What is the number?

_____

The correct answer is **25%**.

■ Practice your skills in reading this line graph. Answer the following questions.

1. In what year did the number of people unemployed begin to decrease?

_____

2. What percent of people were unemployed in 1944?

_____

3. What percent of people were unemployed in 1930?

_____

4. In what year was the number of unemployed people 5%?

_____

5. What percent of people were unemployed in 1937?

_____

6. In what year was there full employment?

_____

Here are the correct answers: **1. 1934**; **2. almost 0%**; **3. 8%**; **4. 1942**; **5. 14%**; **6. 1944**.

By reading this graph, you have learned some important facts and figures about the economic history of the United States. During the 1930s, the poor economy resulted in unemployment for a large percentage of people.

STRATEGY: HOW TO READ A LINE GRAPH

▶ Find the title. What is the topic of the graph?

▶ Read the labels on the bottom and the side of the graph to see what the numbers represent.

▶ Study the entire shape of the line. What changes, or trends, do you notice? Does the line show an increase, a decrease, or both?

▶ Locate different points by reading the numbers on both the bottom and the side of the graph.

▶ Check the relationships between the numbers on the graph.

Exercise 1

Study the line graph and complete the exercise that follows.

Why do more and more women choose to work? How does the economy benefit from working women?

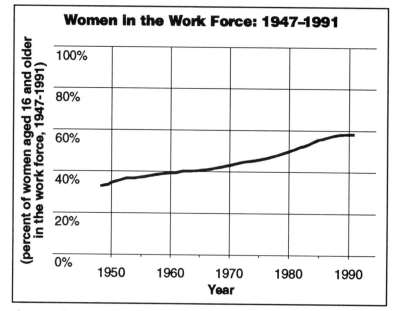

Source: Bureau of Labor Statistics

PART A

Answer the questions in the space provided.

1. What period of time is covered in the graph?

_____

2. What do the numbers on the side of the graph represent?

_____

_____

3. What trend does the graph show?

_____

_____

4. What percent of women worked in 1960?

_____

5. In what year did about 60% of women hold jobs?

_____

6. During what 20-year period did the slowest growth of women in the work force occur?

_____

7. During what 20-year period did the fastest growth of women in the work force occur?

_____

PART B
Circle the best answer for each question.

1. In what year was the number of women in the work force at about 42%?
   (1) 1985
   (2) 1965
   (3) 1990
   (4) 1970

2. About what percent did the number of working women increase from 1980 to 1990?
   (1) 10%
   (2) 40%
   (3) 30%
   (4) 20%

3. In what year did about 45% of women hold jobs?
   (1) 1990
   (2) 1960
   (3) 1975
   (4) 1950

Check your answers on page 162.

Exercise 2

Study the line graph and complete the exercise that follows.

Should the United States government spend more money on education? Or should it spend more money to defend the nation?

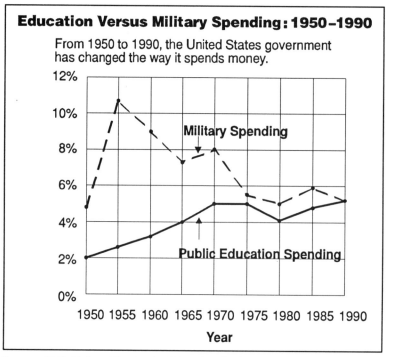

Education Versus Military Spending: 1950–1990

From 1950 to 1990, the United States government has changed the way it spends money.

Source: U.S. National Center for Education Statistics, U.S. Office of Management and Budget

Circle the best answer for each question.

1. During what five-year period did the highest increase in military spending occur?
   - **(1)** 1950 to 1955
   - **(2)** 1965 to 1970
   - **(3)** 1975 to 1980
   - **(4)** 1980 to 1985

2. In what year did education spending begin to decrease?
   - **(1)** 1970
   - **(2)** 1975
   - **(3)** 1980
   - **(4)** 1985

3. What percent was spent on education in 1965?

    (1) 2%

    (2) 4%

    (3) 6%

    (4) 8%

4. What does the graph show about spending in 1990?

    (1) Too much money was spent on education.

    (2) Too little money was spent on the military.

    (3) About the same amount was spent for the military and education.

    (4) Spending for the military has been cut to pay for education.

5. During what five-year period did both military spending and public education spending decrease?

    (1) 1955 to 1960

    (2) 1960 to 1965

    (3) 1970 to 1975

    (4) 1975 to 1980

Check your answers on page 162.

WRITING WORKSHOP

Brainstorm: Write a List

In the early 1990s, many people lost their jobs. How do you think unemployed people feel? What money problems do they face because they can't find work? Write a list describing the effects of being unemployed.

Focus: Write a Topic Sentence

Review your list of effects of unemployment. Choose one effect to write about. Write a topic sentence that states the main point you would like to discuss.

Expand: Write a Paragraph

Develop your topic sentence into a paragraph. Add details that explain one effect of being unemployed.

CHAPTER 17 | BAR GRAPHS

Like most people, you probably enjoy listening to music. How much money do people spend on different types of music? The answer to this question can be shown on a bar graph.

A **bar graph** uses bars to show comparisons and contrasts. In the bar graph shown, the title explains the topic. The labels on the bottom of the bar graph tell you what each bar represents. The label and the numbers on the side of the bar graph help you figure out the height of each bar.

Study the bar graph below. Notice the difference in the heights of the bars.

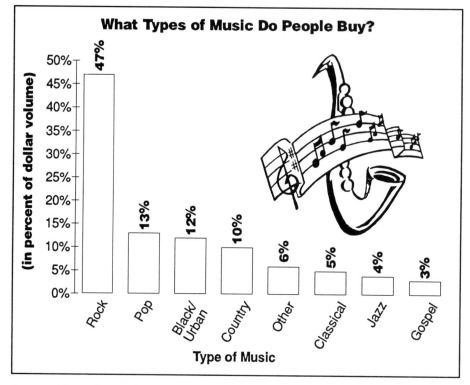

Source: Clinton Research Services

■ Practice your skills in reading the bar graph. Answer the questions below.

1. What type of music is bought the most?

_____

2. What type of music is bought the least?

_____

3. Which type of music represents 10% of music purchased?

_____

4. What percent of people buy classical music?

_____

5. Which type of music do people buy more—country or black/urban?

_____

6. Which type of music represents 13% of music purchased?

_____

7. People who buy pop music represent a higher percentage than which 3 categories?

_____   _____   _____

Here are the answers: **1. rock**; **2. gospel**; **3. country**; **4. 5%**; **5. black/urban**; **6. pop**; **7. classical, jazz, gospel**.

Did you notice that the bar graph helps you compare and contrast information? Bar graphs are used in economics to make the meaning of numbers clearer.

STRATEGY: HOW TO READ A BAR GRAPH

▶ Find the title. What is the topic of the graph?
▶ Read the labels on the bottom of the graph. What does each bar represent?
▶ Read the labels on the side of the graph. What do the numbers represent?
▶ Compare and contrast the height or length of the bars.
▶ Check to see if the heights of the bars represent changes.

Exercise 1

Study the bar graph and complete the exercise that follows.

What groups are entering the work force in greater numbers? How will this increase affect the way companies are run?

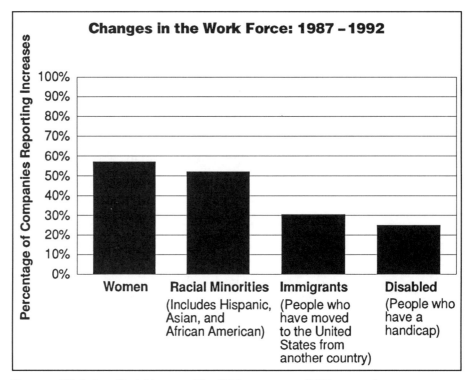

Changes in the Work Force: 1987–1992

Y-axis: Percentage of Companies Reporting Increases

Women — approximately 57%
Racial Minorities (Includes Hispanic, Asian, and African American) — approximately 52%
Immigrants (People who have moved to the United States from another country) — approximately 30%
Disabled (People who have a handicap) — approximately 25%

Source: *Workplace Social Issues of the 1990s,* a survey of 578 companies, © The Olsten Corp., 1992

Answer each question in the space provided.

1. What is the topic of the bar graph?

_____

_____

2. What do the numbers on the left side of the bar graph represent?

_____

3. What four groups of people are represented on the bar graph?

_____   _____

_____   _____

4. What two groups of people have percentages above 50?

_____   _____

5. How are immigrants defined?

_____

_____

6. Which group has the smallest percentage?

_____

7. Which groups are listed under the heading Racial Minorities?

_____ _____ _____

8. What could be a reason for the significant increase of minorities and women in companies' work forces?

_____

Check your answers on page 163.

Exercise 2

Study the bar graph and complete the exercise that follows.

What happens when fathers leave their families? What are the economic effects? What money problems do single mothers face?

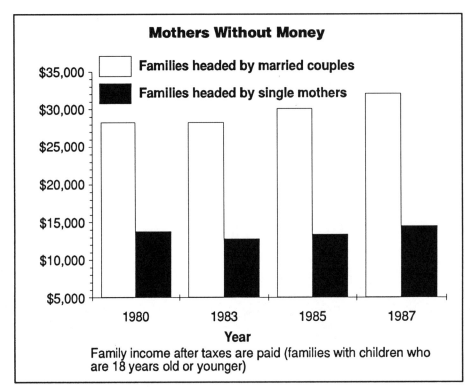

Source: U.S. Bureau of the Census, *Statistical Abstract of the United States: 1991*

Circle the best answer for each question.

1. In what year did families headed by married couples earn the highest income?

   (1) 1980

   (2) 1983

   (3) 1984

   (4) 1987

2. What does the graph show about the incomes of families headed by single mothers during the 1980s?

(1) Incomes steadily increased.

(2) Incomes steadily decreased.

(3) Incomes remained about the same.

(4) Incomes rose sharply and then dropped.

3. During the 1980s, what was the average income of families headed by married couples?

(1) about $15,000

(2) about $20,000

(3) about $25,000

(4) about $28,000

4. What is the comparison shown in the graph?

(1) Families headed by married couples make more than twice as much money as families headed by single mothers.

(2) Twice as many children live in families headed by married couples than in families with single mothers.

(3) Families were better off economically in the early 1980s than the late 1980s.

(4) Mothers who have never divorced earn more money than single mothers.

Check your answers on page 163.

WRITING WORKSHOP

Brainstorm: Ask Questions

Interview someone you know who is a single mother. Prepare a list of questions to ask her about raising her family alone. (*Tip:* Do not ask questions that are too personal.)

Focus: Create a Title

Think of a title that describes the subject of your interview.

Expand: Write the Results of the Interview

Listen carefully and take notes during your interview with a single mother. Write her answer to each interview question.

CHAPTER 18 | CIRCLE GRAPHS

How do you spend your money? What portion of your paycheck do you spend on rent? What portion do you spend on food? A circle graph can help you see how your expenses break down.

A **circle graph** shows how parts relate to a whole. Each portion of the circle graph looks like a slice of a pie. Each "slice," or wedge, of a circle graph is a different size. The circle represents 100 percent. Each wedge of the circle represents an amount less than 100 percent. The wedges should all add up to 100 percent.

The circle graph below shows how the average American spends money. The labels name different kinds of expenses. The numbers show the percentage (%) of each expense. Study the information shown on the circle graph.

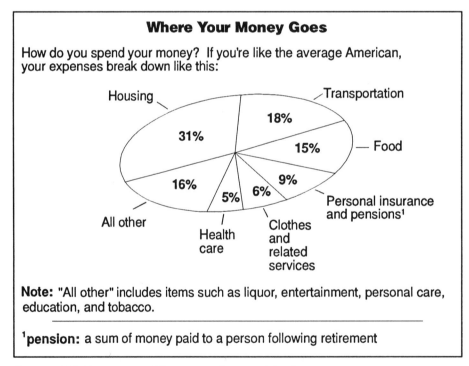

Where Your Money Goes

How do you spend your money? If you're like the average American, your expenses break down like this:

- Housing 31%
- Transportation 18%
- Food 15%
- Personal insurance and pensions[1] 9%
- Clothes and related services 6%
- Health care 5%
- All other 16%

Note: "All other" includes items such as liquor, entertainment, personal care, education, and tobacco.

[1]**pension:** a sum of money paid to a person following retirement

Source: U.S. Department of Commerce, Bureau of the Census

■ Practice your skill in reading the circle graph. Fill in the missing information in the chart below.

Type of Expense	Percentage (%)
Housing	
	18%
Food	
	5%

Compare your answers to the completed chart below.

Type of Expense	Percentage (%)
Housing	31%
Transportation	18%
Food	15%
Health care	5%

The chart summarizes important information found in the circle graph. However, the circle graph gives you a clearer picture of what part of the whole, or total, each percentage represents. A circle graph also helps you see comparisons.

STRATEGY: HOW TO READ A CIRCLE GRAPH

▸ Find the title. What is the topic of the graph?
▸ Read the labels on each portion of the circle. How do the labels relate to the topic of the graph?
▸ Study the percentage (%) and size of each portion. Which portion is largest? Which portion is smallest?
▸ Check to see that each portion adds up to the total (100%).

Exercise 1

Study the circle graph and complete the exercise that follows.

By law, most divorced fathers are supposed to pay money to support their children. Are divorced fathers obeying the law? How are children affected when fathers don't pay child support?

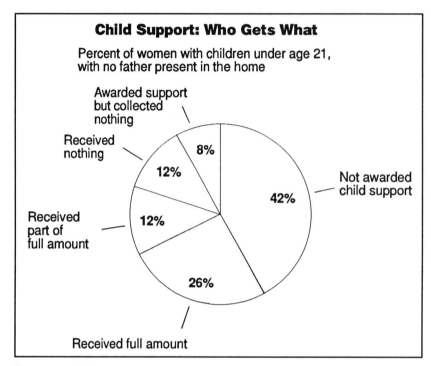

Child Support: Who Gets What

Percent of women with children under age 21, with no father present in the home

- Awarded support but collected nothing
- Received nothing — 12%
- Received part of full amount — 12%
- 8%
- Not awarded child support — 42%
- Received full amount — 26%

Source: U.S. Census Bureau, survey for 1989

Circle the best answer for each question.

1. What is the topic of the graph?
   (1) single mothers
   (2) divorced fathers
   (3) child support
   (4) poor children

2. What percent of mothers have collected the full amount of child support?

    (1) 8%

    (2) 12%

    (3) 20%

    (4) 26%

3. What does the number 42% represent?

    (1) mothers who were not awarded child support

    (2) mothers who are divorced or separated

    (3) mothers who didn't get the full amount of child support

    (4) mothers who were awarded child support but got nothing

4. What percent of mothers received nothing?

    (1) 8%

    (2) 12%

    (3) 26%

    (4) 42%

5. What does the number 8% represent?

    (1) mothers who received the full amount of child support

    (2) mothers who were awarded child support but collected nothing

    (3) mothers who received nothing

    (4) mothers who were not awarded child support

6. What does the graph suggest about fathers who are divorced or separated?

    (1) A large percent care about their children's welfare.

    (2) A small percent are fully supporting their children.

    (3) A small percent can afford child support.

    (4) A large percent regret having children.

Check your answers on page 163.

Exercise 2

Study the circle graph and complete the exercise that follows.

What economic problems do farmers face? Do you think farmers in the United States earn high enough incomes?

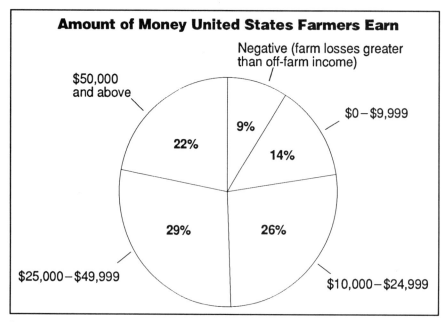

Amount of Money United States Farmers Earn

Negative (farm losses greater than off-farm income)

$50,000 and above

$0–$9,999

9%

22%

14%

29%

26%

$25,000–$49,999

$10,000–$24,999

Source: U.S. Department of Agriculture

Circle the correct answer for each question.

1. What percent of farmers earn $25,000–$49,999?

(1) 9%

(2) 14%

(3) 29%

(4) 26%

2. What does the number 22% represent?

(1) farmers who earn $0–$9,999

(2) farmers who earn $10,000–$24,999

(3) farmers who earn $25,000–$49,999

(4) farmers who earn $50,000 and above

3. What percent of farmers experience farm losses greater than their off-farm income?

    (1) 14%

    (2) 9%

    (3) 22%

    (4) 29%

4. What does the number 14% represent?

    (1) farmers who earn $0–$9,999

    (2) farmers who earn $25,000–$49,999

    (3) farmers who experience farm losses greater than their off-farm income

    (4) farmers who earn $50,000 and above

Check your answers on page 163.

WRITING WORKSHOP

Brainstorm: Make a List

In this chapter, you read a circle graph showing how the average American spends money. What do you spend your money on each month? What bills do you pay? Make a list of your main expenses. Use the list below for ideas:

Rent	Car insurance	Gas	Baby supplies
Food	Health insurance	Phone bill	Entertainment

Focus: Create a Chart

Divide a sheet of paper into two columns. Write "Type of Monthly Expenses" on top of the left-hand column. Write "Amount of Money Spent" on top of the right-hand column.

Expand: Complete the Chart

Refer to your list of monthly expenses as you fill in the chart. Include the cost of each item on your list. Use the list to help budget your money.

UNIT 5
REVIEW

Study the two graphs and complete the exercises that follow.

Where was the car you drive made? What countries produce large numbers of cars? What nations are the leading makers of cars?

PART A
Use the circle graph to answer the questions.

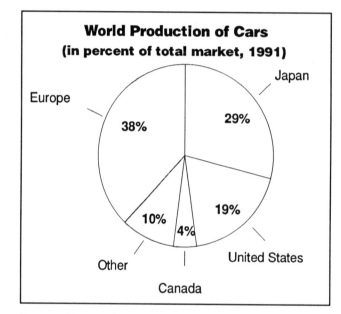

World Production of Cars
(in percent of total market, 1991)

Europe — 38%
Japan — 29%
United States — 19%
Other — 10%
Canada — 4%

Source: Bureau of Labor Statistics, 1991

1. Where were the most cars produced in 1991?
   (1) Canada
   (2) Japan
   (3) Europe
   (4) United States

2. What country ranked third in world production of cars in 1991?
   (1) Canada
   (2) Japan
   (3) Europe
   (4) United States

PART B
Use the line graph to answer the questions.

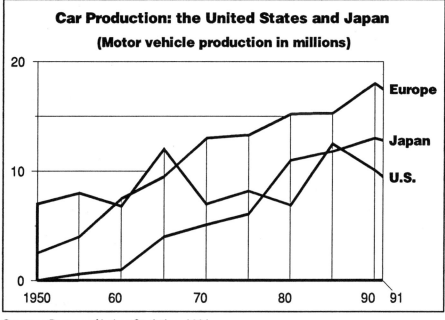

Car Production: the United States and Japan
(Motor vehicle production in millions)

Source: Bureau of Labor Statistics, 1991

1. What trend does the line graph show about the number of cars produced in
Japan between 1950 and 1991?
   (1) Production has increased steadily.
   (2) Production has dropped sharply.
   (3) Production increased slightly and then decreased.
   (4) Production has remained about the same.

2. Which statement best describes the comparison shown in the line graph?
   (1) The United States has always produced more cars than Japan.
   (2) The United States has fallen behind Japan in the number of cars
   produced.
   (3) Japan and the United States have always produced about the same
   number of cars.
   (4) Japan produces cars that are better than those made in the United States.

Check your answers on page 163.

POST-TEST

The post-test will help you check how well you have learned the reading skills in this book. You should take the post-test after you have completed all the chapters in the book.

Read the passage and answer the questions that follow.

How can homeless people find work and hope for their future? What solutions can help the homeless become self-sufficient?

They're Sold on *Streetwise*

There are enough homeless people in Chicago to fill all of the seats in Wrigley Field, where the Chicago Cubs play baseball. A lot of times people don't want to help the homeless, though. Instead, they tell them, "Get a job!" Well, now many of those homeless people are working. Together they are selling *Streetwise*. It is a monthly newspaper written about homeless people. The newspaper helps them make a living. Meanwhile, it raises people's awareness about the homeless.

The first issue came out in September 1992. A month later, more than 375 homeless people found work selling papers. They apply for the job and have an interview. Then the workers must follow these rules: They must wear badges. They must be polite. And, above all, they must never be drunk on the job.

Bill is 23 years old. He lost his home when he lost his job. Like other *Streetwise* workers, he moves around the city. He tries to sell as many papers as he can. "It's a lot of work," says Bill. "I want to work, though. It's just hard to get a job when you don't have an address or a place to wash up." He makes about $30 a day selling *Streetwise*. Bill can afford to rent a room and get off the streets.

Dean Whitaker is the editor of *Streetwise*. He said, "The face of the homeless has really changed. It's you and me out there now." *Streetwise* offers jobs—and hope—for Chicago's homeless.

—adapted from "They're Sold on *Streetwise*," by Brenda Hermann,
Chicago Tribune, October 13, 1992

1. What is the main idea of the passage?
   (1) People who work for *Streetwise* learn important job skills.
   (2) *Streetwise* helps the homeless make a living and raises people's awareness of this problem.
   (3) More than 375 homeless people have found work selling *Streetwise*.
   (4) Bill is a 23-year-old man who lost his job.

2. Based on the passage, what can you infer about the homeless in Chicago?
   (1) Most of Chicago's homeless people live around Wrigley Field.
   (2) Many homeless people in Chicago go to Cubs baseball games.
   (3) Thousands of people in Chicago are homeless.
   (4) Cubs fans don't care about the problems of the homeless.

3. According to the passage, why do many people avoid helping the homeless?
   (1) They feel that the homeless are rude.
   (2) They believe that the homeless don't want jobs.
   (3) They think that the homeless have a drinking problem.
   (4) They think that the homeless have a mental problem.

4. Which statement best summarizes Dean Whitaker's remark?
   (1) People from all backgrounds are among today's homeless.
   (2) The faces of homeless people are filled with sadness.
   (3) *Streetwise* has changed the lives of homeless people.
   (4) Many people are out on the streets looking for jobs.

5. Which statement best summarizes the rules *Streetwise* workers must follow?
   (1) Workers must wear name tags, be courteous, and stay sober while they are working.
   (2) Workers must move around the city and sell a certain number of newspapers each day.
   (3) Workers must rent a room and get off the streets.
   (4) Workers must wash up and have a home address.

6. Which detail is *not* given in the article?
   (1) Dean Whitaker is the editor of *Streetwise*.
   (2) The first issue of *Streetwise* came out in September 1990.
   (3) Workers can make $30 a day selling *Streetwise*.
   (4) A month after *Streetwise* came out, more than 375 homeless found work selling papers.

Read the passage and answer the questions that follow.

What role did African Americans play in settling the West? What risks did they take in order to gain freedom?

African-American Pioneers

Journey back in time to a place called the Wild West. Meet a brave man and woman who blazed new trails. The word *pioneer* refers to someone who breaks new ground. A pioneer paves new paths for others to follow. This is certainly true for African Americans who went west during the 1800s. The chance to gain their freedom made them risk this dangerous trip.

A man named York was one of those pioneers. He was born into slavery in Virginia. He was a childhood friend of William Clark, a famous explorer. Clark was one of the leaders of the famous Lewis and Clark expedition. The trip, which lasted from 1804 to 1806, was the first U.S. overland journey to the Pacific coast and back. York was Clark's guide during this dangerous journey. York acted very bravely. As a result, Clark gave York his freedom. Later, York became chief of the Crow Indians.

Biddy Mason also found freedom in the West. Her journey began in 1851. She walked from Mississippi to California behind a wagon train. She arrived in California a year later. Slavery was against the law in this state. Mason sued her master. She finally won her freedom. She settled in Los Angeles. In time, she owned businesses and land. By the late 1860s, Mason became a rich and well-known woman.

These are two of the many forgotten pioneers in history. They escaped slavery in the South and realized their dreams of freedom.

7. According to the passage, what caused many African-American pioneers to go west during the 1800s?
   (1) the promise of wealth
   (2) the hope for freedom
   (3) the sense of adventure
   (4) the chance for fame

8. The details in the second paragraph focus on the experiences of
   (1) Lewis
   (2) Clark
   (3) York
   (4) Crow Indians

9. What happened to Biddy Mason in 1851?
   (1) She left Mississippi following a wagon train.
   (2) She arrived in California.
   (3) She sued her master.
   (4) She became a wealthy woman.

10. You can infer from the passage that the most important trait of a pioneer is
    (1) business ability
    (2) knowledge
    (3) courage
    (4) helpfulness

11. Which event mentioned about York in the article happened last?
    (1) York won his freedom.
    (2) York was born into slavery in Virginia.
    (3) York became chief of the Crow Indians.
    (4) York acted as a guide on the Lewis and Clark expedition.

12. What happened to Mason as a result of suing her master?
    (1) She won her freedom.
    (2) She was able to own land.
    (3) She was able to start her own business.
    (4) all of the above

Read the passage and answer the questions that follow.

Do TV debates affect the way you vote? How did TV viewers react to the first TV debate?

The Kennedy-Nixon Debates

In the fall of 1960, millions of voters watched the candidates for president talk about important issues. This was the first TV debate in American history.

John F. Kennedy was the Democratic candidate for president. He faced two problems. The first was his age. He was only forty-three years old. Second, he had less experience than the Republican candidate, Vice President Richard Nixon. To overcome these problems, Kennedy challenged Nixon to a TV debate. Nixon accepted the challenge. On September 26, the two candidates stood before the TV cameras.

TV viewers noticed differences between these two men right away. Kennedy was more handsome. He seemed relaxed and full of energy. In contrast, Nixon looked pale, tired, and nervous. He needed a shave. His makeup made him look bad.

Kennedy attacked Nixon right away. He listed Nixon's failures. Nixon defended himself with skill. He talked about his experience in handling Nikita Khrushchev, the Soviet leader. However, Nixon's remarks did not excite the voters.

During the debate, Nixon made his comments to Kennedy. However, Kennedy spoke directly to the TV viewers. This is one reason viewers thought Kennedy was the winner.

Later, the Democrats made a commercial from the debate. It showed Kennedy answering questions with great confidence. Then it showed Nixon's reaction. He was sweating and frowning.

The polls predicted a very close election. These predictions came true. Some political experts believed that the first TV debate was the reason for Kennedy's narrow victory. Kennedy agreed with their opinion. He said, "We wouldn't have had a prayer without [television]."

13. How did Kennedy solve his problems as a Democratic candidate for president?

    (1) He ran TV commercials to gain votes.

    (2) He challenged Nixon to a TV debate.

    (3) He asked political experts their opinions.

    (4) He listed Nixon's failures as vice president.

14. What difference between Kennedy and Nixon made TV viewers think that Kennedy won the debate?

    (1) Kennedy was more handsome.

    (2) Kennedy appeared more relaxed.

    (3) Kennedy was full of energy.

    (4) Kennedy spoke directly to the TV viewers.

15. According to the passage, which of the following was an opinion of political experts?

    (1) Kennedy was too young to be a good president.

    (2) Nixon had experience with the leader of the Soviet Union.

    (3) The TV debate was the reason for Kennedy's victory.

    (4) Nixon defended Kennedy's attacks with skill.

16. Given the information in the passage, you might predict that

    (1) the outcome of TV debates will continue to affect voters' decisions.

    (2) Democratic candidates for president will keep winning TV debates.

    (3) Republican candidates for president will improve their debating skills.

    (4) elections for president will continue to be very close races.

17. According to the passage, what two factors did Kennedy have to overcome during his TV debate with Nixon?

    (1) his lack of ease and his unattractive image

    (2) his tendency to sweat and his frequent frowning

    (3) his youth and his lack of experience

    (4) his unexciting delivery and his inability to look his opponent in the eye.

18. Given the description of how Nixon and Kennedy performed in their TV debate, you might predict that

    (1) Nixon would win the debate.

    (2) Nixon's and Kennedy's performances would be considered equal.

    (3) Kennedy would win the debate.

    (4) none of the above

Use the map and the notes to answer the questions that follow.

Where did the United States fight battles with Mexico? What paths did United States troops take during the Mexican War?

The Mexican War

Background notes: From 1846 to 1848, the United States and Mexico fought a war. At the end of the war, the United States paid Mexico 15 million dollars for a large area of land from Texas to the Pacific Ocean. General Zachary Taylor, Colonel Philip Kearny, and General Winfield Scott were leaders of the United States troops. The map below shows the movement of their troops. It also shows the locations of American and Mexican victories.

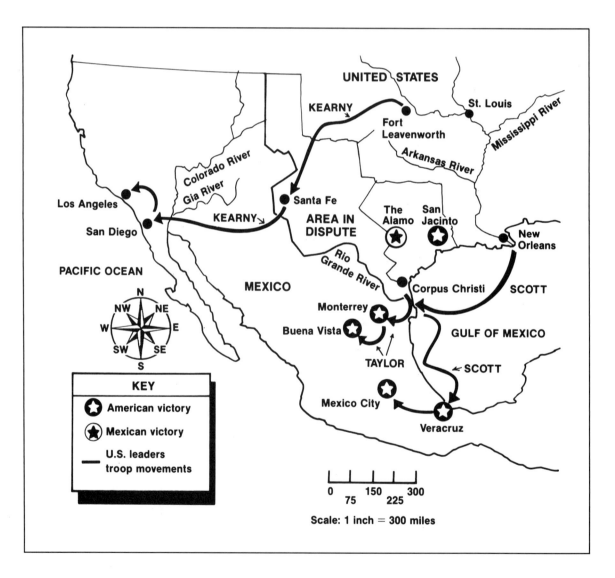

19. In which of the following places was there a Mexican victory?

   (1) San Antonio

   (2) Buena Vista

   (3) the Alamo

   (4) San Jacinto

20. In which direction did Colonel Kearny's troops move after they stopped at Sante Fe?

   (1) north

   (2) southwest

   (3) east

   (4) west

21. About how many miles did General Scott's troops travel from Veracruz to Mexico City?

   (1) about 75 miles

   (2) about 150 miles

   (3) about 225 miles

   (4) over 300 miles

22. Where did Zachary Taylor's troops go right after Corpus Christi?

   (1) Monterrey

   (2) New Orleans

   (3) Mexico City

   (4) Buena Vista

23. According to the map, which country had more victories during the Mexican War—the United States or Mexico?

   _____

24. About how many miles is Fort Leavenworth from Santa Fe?

   (1) 200

   (2) 100

   (3) 300

   (4) 500

Study the line graphs and answer the questions that follow.

In the late 1980s, the United States economy began to weaken. How has the bad economy affected family life in the United States? Why do money problems change people's decisions about getting married and having children?

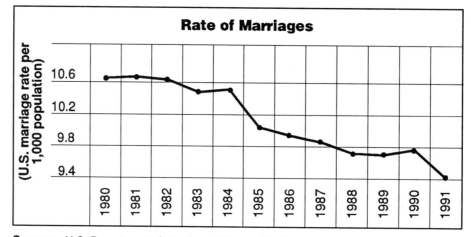

Source: U.S. Department of Health and Human Services

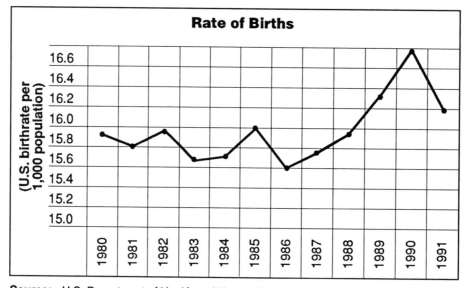

Source: U.S. Department of Health and Human Services

25. During what period of time did marriage rates remain unchanged?

    (1) from 1980 to 1982

    (2) from 1982 to 1984

    (3) from 1984 to 1986

    (4) from 1986 to 1988

26. What was the rate of birth in 1986?

    (1) 15.4

    (2) 15.6

    (3) 15.8

    (4) 16

27. During what period of time did the sharpest increase of births occur?

    (1) from 1982 to 1983

    (2) from 1984 to 1985

    (3) from 1985 to 1986

    (4) from 1988 to 1989

28. What trend do the two line graphs show as a result of the bad economy in 1990?

    (1) a sharp drop in both the number of marriages and births

    (2) a slight decrease in marriages and an increase in births

    (3) an increase in marriages and a decrease in births

    (4) a steady increase in both the number of marriages and births

29. From 1986 to 1988, the rate of births increased and the rate of marriages

    (1) stayed the same

    (2) increased

    (3) decreased

    (4) went up and down

30. Which fact do you learn from reading the second chart?

    (1) The rate of births decreased from 1989 to 1990.

    (2) The rate of births increased from 1985 to 1986.

    (3) The rate of births decreased from 1983 to 1984.

    (4) The rate of births went up and down from 1984 to 1986.

Check your answers on page 154.

POST-TEST ANSWER KEY

1. **(2)** The last two sentences of the first paragraph state the main idea of the passage—that *Streetwise* helps the homeless make a living and raises people's awareness of this problem.

2. **(3)** Wrigley Field holds several thousand fans. Imagine all the seats of a baseball park completely filled with homeless people. The first sentence suggests their huge numbers.

3. **(2)** The first paragraph states "A lot of times people don't want to help the homeless, though. Instead, they tell them, 'Get a job!' "

4. **(1)** This choice summarizes the meaning of Whitaker's remark: "The face of the homeless has really changed. It's you and me out there now." In other words, anyone can become homeless.

5. **(1)** This choice is a summary of the rules stated in paragraph 2.

6. **(2)** *Streetwise* first came out in September 1992.

7. **(2)** The last sentence of the first paragraph states this cause.

8. **(3)** The details in the second paragraph support the topic sentence: "A man named York was one of those pioneers."

9. **(1)** The second and third sentences of the third paragraph explain the event that occurred in 1851.

10. **(3)** Clues that support this inference are mentioned in the first paragraph. For example, the word "brave" and the phrase "risk this dangerous trip" suggest that a pioneer must have courage.

11. **(3)** York became a chief of the Crow Indians after he was born into slavery **(2)**, acted as a guide on the Lewis and Clark expedition **(4)**, and won his freedom **(1)**.

12. **(4)** As a result of Mason suing her master, she won her freedom **(1)**, was able to own land **(2)**, and had an opportunity to start her own business **(3)**.

13. **(2)** The fifth sentence of the second paragraph states this solution to Kennedy's problems.

14. **(4)** The fifth paragraph explains this key difference between Kennedy and Nixon.

15. **(3)** The last paragraph states this opinion of political experts.

16. **(1)** The passage states that millions of voters watched this first TV debate. Kennedy and some political experts believed the debate played a key role in the election. Therefore, you can predict that TV debates will continue to affect voters' decisions. For example, this prediction was true during the 1992 election for president.

17. **(3)** Choices **(1)**, **(2)**, and **(4)** are factors that affected Nixon's, not Kennedy's, performance during the TV debate.

18. **(3)** According to the article, Kennedy's ease in front of a camera, his energy, good presentation, and ability to speak to viewers directly would lead to the prediction that Kennedy might win the debate over Nixon.

19. **(3)** The symbol next to the Alamo, as shown on the map key, means a Mexican victory.

20. **(2)** The arrow on the map points toward the left and down, which is the direction southwest (SW).

21. **(3)** According to the map scale, the distance is about 225 miles.

22. **(1)** As shown on the map, the arrow after Corpus Christi points to Monterrey.

23. the United States

24. **(4)** The mileage key shows that 1 inch = 300 miles, so the correct distance is a little over 500 miles.

25. **(1)** The line between the years 1980 to 1982 goes straight across. This shows that the marriage rate for this time period did not change.

26. **(2)** The point on the line graph for 1986 is 15.6.

27. **(4)** The line on the graph climbs straight up from less than 15.9 to 16.3. As the graph shows, the sharpest increase in the birthrate occurred during this time period.

28. **(1)** In both graphs, the line drops sharply in 1990.

29. **(3)** The rate of marriages decreased during the period from 1986 to 1988.

30. **(4)** According to the chart, the rate of births went up and down during the period from 1984 to 1986.

POST-TEST EVALUATION CHART

Use the answer key on page 154 to check your answers to the Post-Test. Then find the item number of each question you missed and circle it on the chart below. Next, write the number of correct answers you had for each skill. If you need more practice in any skill, refer back to the chapter that covers that skill area.

Chapter	Skill	Item Numbers	Number Correct
1	Main idea	1, 8	＿＿
2	Supporting details	3, 6	＿＿
3	Summarizing	4, 5	＿＿
4	Sequence	9, 11	＿＿
5	Cause and Effect	7, 12	＿＿
6	Problem and Solution	13, 17	＿＿
7	Comparison and Contrast	14, 23, 29	＿＿
8	Facts and Opinions	15, 30	＿＿
9	Inferences	2, 10	＿＿
10	Predicting outcomes	16, 18	＿＿
12	Map keys	19, 22	＿＿
13	Directions and Distances on a Map	20, 21, 24	＿＿
16	Line Graphs	25, 26, 27, 28	＿＿

ANSWER KEY

Unit 1: Behavioral Sciences
Chapter 1: Finding the Main Idea
Exercise 1, pages 6–7

1. **(2)** The entire passage focuses on this topic. The other answers relate to or support the main topic of older people.

2. **(2)** Choice **(1)** is not true. Choices **(3)** and **(4)** tell you more about the main idea.

3. **(4)** The definition of *anthropologist* is given in the passage.

4. **(2)** This choice states why older workers are valuable.

5. **(2)** Mead was 72 when she studied the people of New Guinea again. The other choices are given in the passage.

6. **(4)** Picasso died at the age of 91. The other choices are given in the passage.

Exercise 2, pages 8–9

1. **(2)** The title of the passage tells you that the topic is skinheads.

2. **(4)** Choices **(1)**, **(2)**, and **(3)** tell you more about the main idea.

3. **(1)** The topic sentence is the first sentence of the paragraph. Choices **(2)**, **(3)**, and **(4)** tell you more about the main idea.

Chapter 2: Finding Details
Exercise 1, pages 12–13

1. **(1)** The first sentence of the passage tells you when the lunar new year occurs.

2. **(4)** The second sentence of the third paragraph tells you this detail.

3. **(3)** The last sentence of the passage tells you this detail.

Exercise 2, pages 14–15

Answers may vary. Use these answers as a guideline.
1. both men and women

2. from a mother infected with HIV

3. hugs, handshakes, kisses, or mosquitoes

4. don't have sex, or have sex with only one partner who isn't infected

5. by sharing needles

Chapter 3: Restating and Summarizing
Exercise 1, pages 18–19

1. **(3)** All the details in the passage relate to the topic of superstitious baseball players.

2. **(2)** This is the only sentence that explains the meaning of the last sentence of the second paragraph.

3. **(2)** This choice restates the topic sentence, which summarizes the main idea of the paragraph. The topic sentence is the first sentence of the third paragraph.

4. **(1), (3), (4)** Choices **(1)**, **(3)**, and **(4)** are mentioned in the passage. Choices **(2)** and **(5)** are not.

Exercise 2, pages 20–21

Answers may vary. Use these answers as a guideline.
1. A mother works to help support her family. Her family needs the money she earns from her job.

2. Every morning, Peter irons his own clothes, Pat works out, and their daughter watches cartoon shows.

3. **(3)** Choice **(3)** is mentioned in the passage. Choices **(1)**, **(2)**, and **(4)** are not.

Unit 1 Review, pages 22–23

1. **(1)** This is the main idea of the paragraph. The other choices are details that relate to the main idea.

2. **(2)** This definition means the same thing as "value as a human being."

3. **(4)** This detail is *not* mentioned in the third paragaph.

4. **(4)** Etheridge Knight stated that "I died from a prison sentence, and poetry brought me back to life."

5. **(2)** None of the other choices is true based on the article.

Unit 2: U.S. History
Chapter 4: Sequence
Exercise 1, pages 28–29

Answers may vary. Use these answers as a guideline.
1. December 17, 1903   Wright brothers' flight in first successful plane

   May 20, 1927   Charles Lindbergh's nonstop, solo flight across the Atlantic Ocean

   May 20, 1932   Amelia Earhart's nonstop, solo flight across the Atlantic Ocean

2. Earhart, like Lindbergh, made a solo, nonstop flight across the Atlantic Ocean. She was the first woman to do so.

3. It made history because it was the first successful flight made in an airplane.

Exercise 2, pages 30–31

The correct time order of the statements is 3, 2, 4, 6, 1, 5.

Chapter 5: Cause and Effect
Exercise 1, pages 34–35

PART A

1. **(2)** The last sentence of the second paragraph states this cause.

2. **(1)** The topic sentence is the first sentence of the paragraph. It states the cause-and-effect relationship. Choices **(2)**, **(3)**, and **(4)** tell you more information about the topic sentence.

3. **(4)** The eighth sentence of the last paragraph states this cause. The clue words *As a result* begin the sentence.

PART B

1. $2.00

2. **(a)** dirty, **(b)** unsafe, **(c)** overcrowded

Exercise 2, pages 36–37

PART A

1. cause, effect

2. cause, effect

3. effect, cause

4. cause, effect

5. effect, cause

PART B

1. **(3)** The whole passage explains why the West was so wild.

2. **(4)** This choice is stated in the fourth and fifth sentences of paragraph 3.

Exercise 3, pages 38–39

PART A

1. **(3)** The first sentence of the passage states the purpose, or main idea, of the passage.

2. **(2)** The first sentence of the second paragraph states the cause.

3. **(4)** The third paragraph states this bad effect. According to the passage, choices **(1)**, **(2)**, and **(3)** are not bad effects.

PART B

Good Effects	Bad Effects
(1) roads connect city and country	**(1)** car accidents
(2) people could take long trips	**(2)** traffic jams and street noise
(3) tourism grew	**(3)** sexual promiscuity
	(4) "getaway" cars

Chapter 6: Problem and Solution
Exercise 1, pages 42–43

1. **(3)** The first sentence of the third paragraph states that drinking was the problem.

2. **(2)** The third paragraph states that the Eighteenth Amendment was the solution to the problem of drinking.

3. **(4)** The third sentence of the fifth paragraph states this effect.

4. **(1)** The author makes this point in the first and last sentences of the second paragraph.

Exercise 2, pages 44–45

Answers may vary. Use these answers as a guideline.
1. cotton

2. The Cherokees occupied valuable land where cotton was grown.

3. The Indian Removal Act required Native Americans to give up their land. In exchange, they would move to new territories west of the Mississippi.

4. President Jackson thought the act was a fair solution to a difficult problem. He felt the Cherokees would be in a better situation.

5. The Cherokees refused to leave Georgia.

6. The "Trail of Tears" was the forced march of the Cherokees to Arkansas in which about 4,000 Cherokees died along the way.

Exercise 3, pages 46–47

1. **T** The first two sentences of the passage state this information (paragraph 2, sentence 2).

2. **F** The first problem Roosevelt solved was the banking problem (paragraph 2, sentence 4).

3. **F** During the "bank holiday," Roosevelt closed the banks for four days.

4. **T** The second paragraph explains the Emergency Banking Act.

5. **T** This statement summarizes Roosevelt's first quotation in the third paragraph.

6. **F** When the banks reopened, people went to them to deposit their savings (paragraph 3, sentence 6).

7. **F** Roosevelt admitted that his solutions might not always work (paragraph 4, sentence 4).

Chapter 7: Comparison and Contrast
Exercise 1, pages 50–51

Answers may vary. Use these answers as a guideline.

	Rosie the Riveter	June Cleaver
1.	1940s	1950s
2.	overalls	dresses, pearls, high heels
3.	building war planes, ships, and army tanks	cleaning the house and being a mother and wife
4.	factory	home
5.	to preserve freedom	to preserve family life

Exercise 2, pages 52–53
PART A

1. **F** The newspaper article praised Lincoln's handling of the war (paragraph 2, sentence 2).

2. **F** The first sentence of the fourth paragraph states that Lincoln might not be accepted as a leader today.

3. **T** The fifth paragraph states this detail.

4. **F** The Bible was Lincoln's source of inner strength (paragraph 4, sentence 2).

5. **T** The last paragraph makes this point.

PART B

(c) Lincoln might not be considered smooth or polished enough to run for office today.

Exercise 3, pages 54–55

1. **(2)** The first sentence of the passage states that both Washington and DuBois shared this concern.

2. **(1)** The fourth sentence of the third paragraph makes this comparison.

3. **(3)** The first sentence of the last paragraph states this difference.

Unit 2 Review, pages 56–57

1. **(2)** The first sentence of the second paragraph states this similarity.

2. **(1)** The first and second sentences of the third paragraph state these events.

3. **(2)** The third sentence of the fifth paragraph explains that this act was passed to help owners capture runaway slaves.

4. **(4)** The last sentence of the passage states this effect.

Unit 3: Political Science
Chapter 8: Fact and Opinion
Exercise 1, pages 62–63
PART A

1. **F** (paragraph 2, sentence 1)

2. **O** This statement cannot be proved.

3. F (paragraph 4, sentences 2–3)

4. O This statement cannot be proved.

5. F (paragraph 4, sentence 8)

6. F (paragraph 5, sentence 6)

7. O This statement cannot be proved.

PART B

(3), (5) The other choices are not true in a democracy.

Exercise 2, pages 64–65

1. **(4)** This statement cannot be proved true.

2. **(3)** The seventh sentence of the second paragraph states Karl Marx's opinion.

3. **(1)** The eighth sentence of paragraph 6 explains Khrushchev's opinion.

4. **(2)** The fifth paragraph details this fact.

Exercise 3, pages 66–67

1. **F** (paragraph 2, sentence 2)

2. **O** This statement cannot be proved.

3. **O** This statement cannot be proved.

4. **F** (paragraph 5, sentence 2)

5. **F** (paragraph 6, sentence 3)

6. **O** This statement cannot be proved.

7. **F**

Chapter 9: Inferences
Exercise 1, pages 70–71

1. **(2)** Each sentence quoted by Mark Brown has clues that support this inference. The other answers are not inferences based on the entire quotation.

2. **(2)** The second paragraph states these three presidents were clear examples of Democrats. "They knew what being a Democrat was all about." No clues in the passage support the other answers.

3. **(1)** The first sentence of the last paragraph tells you that Republican presidents were elected in the 1980s. This clue supports the inference.

4. **(2)** Mark Brown wants the pattern of electing Republican presidents to change. Therefore, you can infer that "right messenger" means a Democratic president. The "right message" means a clear definition of the word *Democrat*.

5. **(1), (3), (5)** The other choices are not goals of today's Democrats.

Exercise 2, pages 72–73

1. **(2)** The details in the passage all relate to this point.

2. **(2)** The lawyer's comments show that she is on the bosses' side. Therefore, you can infer that she would defend their rights.

3. **(3)** The passage tells you that for every worker who wins a case, 300 lose. This clue supports the inference.

4. **(4)** The other choices are not true of most employers.

Exercise 3, pages 74–75

Answers may vary. Use these answers as a guideline.

1. **Clues:** Children go trick-or-treating for UNICEF. During Christmas, people send UNICEF greeting cards.

2. **Clues:** The General Assembly of the United Nations voted to keep UNICEF active. It wanted to help poor children with food, homes, education, and health care.

3. **Clues:** UNICEF trains parents to care for their children's health and safety.

4. **Clues:** UNICEF workers look for cheap, healthy foods for poor children. In Algeria, UNICEF invented a powder to mix with other foods. It also made a mix of salts for sick babies.

Chapter 10: Predicting Outcomes
Exercise 1, pages 78–79

1. **(1)** The list of nations supports this main point.

2. **(3)** The fifth sentence of the fourth paragraph states this outcome.

3. **(2)** The last sentence of the fifth paragraph makes this prediction.

4. (3) The article mentions South Africa as one of four nations believed to have a store of nuclear weapons.

Exercise 2, pages 80–81

Answers may vary. Use these answers as a guideline.

PART A

1. (3) The headline reads, "Yes, Delores Is a Guard."

PART B

1. The Supreme Court of Washington ruled that girls had the right to play on a school's football team. Denying that right was "sex discrimination."

2. They predicted that all school athletics might end.

3. Answers will vary. Reasons should support the prediction.

Exercise 3, pages 82–83

1. (2) The third sentence of the first paragraph states this cause.

2. (2) The sixth sentence of the third paragraph explains why TV affects the outcome of an election.

3. (1) The last paragraph gives you details about TV campaigns. "This stops better candidates from running" supports the prediction.

Chapter 11: Political Cartoons
Exercise 1, pages 86–87

1. because health care costs are too expensive for many Americans to afford

2. because medical insurance costs too much money

3. health care for the poor

4. federal cutbacks; state cutbacks

5. The two men have removed the wheels.

6. The man in the wheelchair is left helpless.

7. Answers will vary. Use this answer as a guideline: Poor people will suffer like the man in the wheelchair. The government won't help them. They won't have money to pay for health problems or medical treatment.

Exercise 2, pages 88–89

1. Possible answers: USA shorts ($6.75); socks ($9.12); cap ($17.25).

2. dollar signs; to show the man's greed

3. counting his cash

4. WAR IS $ELL!

5. to show that he is making a lot of money

6. Answers will vary. Use this answer as a guideline: The man's business takes advantage of Desert Storm (the Persian Gulf War). His store is filled with Desert Storm products. He sees the war as a way to make a lot of money.

Exercise 3, pages 90–91

1. corporate America

2. He is a fat, bald man wearing a business suit and tie. He is smoking a cigar. His hands are open.

3. "WHITE MALES"; "WOMEN & MINORITIES"

4. a fancy office

5. a broom closet

6. Answers will vary. Use this answer as a guideline: No, he is telling a lie. White men have a much better chance to succeed in business. Women and minorities get stuck with low-paying jobs.

Unit 3 Review, pages 92–93
PART A

1. (2) The author makes this inference in the last sentence of the first paragraph.

2. (4) This statement cannot be proved true.

3. (1) This prediction is stated in the third sentence of the last paragraph.

PART B

1. (3) Terrorists need an audience so their demands can be heard.

2. (2) The terrorist is looking right into the TV camera. His mouth is opened as though he is speaking. These details support this opinion.

Unit 4: Geography
Chapter 12: Map Keys
Exercise 1, pages 98–99

1. Dallas, Denver, Rapid City

2. San Francisco, Los Angeles, Minneapolis, New York, Miami

3. Seattle, Atlanta

4. Seattle, Rapid City

5. 77

6. 73

7. Denver

8. Answers will vary.

Exercise 2, pages 100–101

1. (1) The map shows that about one-fourth of Arizona's area is covered by federal Indian reservations.

2. (1) A circle on the map represents Indian groups living outside of reservations. Oregon is marked with the fewest circles.

3. (3) A triangle on the map represents state reservations. New York is marked with the most triangles.

Chapter 13: Finding Directions and Distances
Exercise 1, pages 104–105

1. Texas

2. north

3. about 1,300 miles

4. about 450 miles

5. Maine, Connecticut, Rhode Island

6. about 1,500 miles

7. Texas

8. Oklahoma, Illinois, North Carolina, Pennsylvania

Exercise 2, pages 106–107

1. south

2. Alabama, Mississippi, Louisiana

3. 225 miles

4. 175 miles

5. 375 miles

6. 175 miles

7. 200 miles

Chapter 14: Historical Maps
Exercise 1, pages 110–111

1. when women gained the right to vote

2. to add an amendment to the Constitution that would give women the right to vote

3. (a) Colorado, Idaho, Utah, Washington, California, Arizona, Kansas, Oregon, Montana, Nevada, Wyoming
   (b) west

4. Illinois

5. Texas, Missouri, Arkansas, Indiana, Tennessee, Florida, Alabama, Georgia, South Carolina, North Carolina, Virginia, West Virginia, Maryland, Pennsylvania, Maine

Exercise 2, pages 112–113

1. 19

2. 3

3. Monterey

4. San Diego, San Francisco, San Jose

5. almost 200 miles

6. about 75 miles

Unit 4 Review, pages 114–115

1. (4) The map shows that the Goodnight-Loving Trail is the longest cattle trail on the map.

2. (1) The railroad line labeled on the California coast is the Southern Pacific.

3. (3) Using the map scale, you can estimate that the distance is about 500 miles.

4. (2) The map shows three railroad lines leading to and from Chicago

5. (3) The map shows that San Antonio was connected to four cattle trails.

6. (4) The Shawnee Trail ended in Kansas City.

Unit 5: Economics
Chapter 15: Charts
Exercise 1, pages 120–121

1. **F** By comparing the numbers in both columns, you can see a big difference between the percentages for each job characteristic.

2. **T** 81% rate good health insurance as very important; 56% rate high salary as very important.

3. **F** 66% rate a yearly vacation of one week or more as very important; 58% rate regular hours as very important.

4. **T** The percentages under "Completely Satisfied" range from 13% to 46%.

5. **T** The numbers are 52% and 45%. The gaps between other pairs of numbers are greater.

6. **T** Both interesting work and job security are rated at 78%.

7. **F** 58% rate limited job stress as very important.

8. **T** Both job security and yearly vacation time are rated at 35%.

9. **F** 68% rate the chance to learn new job skills as very important. Therefore, you can infer that 68% of the workers would also consider job training as important.

10. **F** If employers were meeting workers' needs, the percentages in the second column of numbers would be much higher.

11. **F** 68% of workers feel that learning new skills is very important, while 62% of workers feel recognition by co-workers is very important.

12. **T** 34% of workers do feel they are doing work that can help others.

Exercise 2, pages 122–123

1. $7,100,000

2. Nolan Ryan

3. Ryne Sandberg and Roger Clemens

4. Bobby Bonilla and Dwight Gooden

5. Kirby Puckett

6. $5,425,000

7. Athletics

8. $3,000,000

9. George Foster and Jose Canseco

10. Roger Clemens

Chapter 16: Line Graphs
Exercise 1, pages 126–127

PART A

1. 1947 to 1991

2. Percent of women aged 16 or older in the work force

3. The number of working women has grown steadily since 1947.

4. 40%

5. 1990

6. 1950 to 1970

7. 1970 to 1990

PART B

1. 1965

2. 10%

3. 1975

Exercise 2, pages 128–129

1. **(1)** The line graph shows that the highest increase in military spending occurred from 1950 to 1955.

2. **(2)** The line graph shows a decrease from about 1975 to 1980.

3. **(2)** The line graph shows that 4% was spent on education in 1965.

4. **(3)** The two lines on the graph are almost at the same point in the year 1990. There is not enough information on the graph to support the other choices.

5. **(4)** The line graph shows that both military spending and public education spending decreased from 1975 to 1980.

Chapter 17: Bar Graphs
Exercise 1, pages 132–133

1. changes in the work force

2. percentages of companies reporting increases

3. women, racial minorities, immigrants, disabled

4. women, racial minorities

5. as people who have moved to the United States from another country

6. disabled

7. Hispanic, Asian, and African-American

8. Answers will vary, but affirmative action programs and equal opportunity goals can be named as contributing factors.

Exercise 2, pages 134–135

1. **(4)** The bar representing 1987 is the tallest. It is above the $30,000 mark.

2. **(3)** Each bar for incomes of families headed by single mothers is roughly the same height. The bars for 1980, 1983, and 1985 show incomes slightly under $15,000. The bar for 1987 is about $14,000.

3. **(4)** The bars for incomes of families headed by married couples are either slightly under or slighly over $30,000. Therefore, you can estimate that about $28,000 was the average income during the 1980s.

4. **(1)** The bar graph shows that families headed by married couples have over twice the income compared to families headed by single mothers (2 × $15,000 = $30,000). The comparisons explained in the other answers are not shown on the bar graph.

Chapter 18: Circle Graphs
Exercise 1, pages 138–139

1. **(3)** The title of the graph states this topic.

2. **(4)** The label on the graph "Received full amount" points to the portion marked 26%.

3. **(1)** The label on graph "Not awarded child support" points to the portion marked 42%.

4. **(2)** The graph shows that 12% of the mothers received nothing.

5. **(2)** The number 8% represents mothers who were awarded child support but collected nothing.

6. **(2)** By looking closely at the different portions of the circle graph, you can see that 26% is a small part compared to the whole. Therefore, you can infer that only a small percentage of divorced or separated fathers are fully supporting their children. The other choices are not supported by the information shown in the graph.

Exercise 2, pages 140–141

1. **(3)** 29%

2. **(4)** The number 22% represents farmers who earn $50,000 and above.

3. **(2)** 9%

4. **(1)** The number 14% represents farmers who earn $0–$9,999.

Unit 5 Review, pages 142–143
PART A

1. **(3)** The largest portion of the circle graph (38%) represents Europe.

2. **(4)** The third largest portion of the circle graph (19%) represents the United States.

PART B

1. **(1)** The line labeled "Japan" rises fairly steadily from 0 cars in 1950 to almost 15 million cars in 1991.

2. **(2)** In the late 1970s, the line labeled "United States" drops beneath the line labeled "Japan." This drop shows that the United States is no longer producing as many cars as Japan.